The World
of Dance

The World of Dance

MELVIN BERGER

S. G. Phillips, Inc. New York

Library of Congress Cataloging in Publication Data

Berger, Melvin.
    The world of dance.

    Bibliography: p.
    Includes index.
    1. Dancing—History—Juvenile literature.
I. Title.
GV1601.B47   793.3'19   78-14498
ISBN 0-87599-221-8

For Dan Wagoner

ACKNOWLEDGMENTS

Many people helped me with the writing of this book. I am grateful to all of them. I would like, however, to express my particular appreciation to the following organizations and people, who provided me with much information and many excellent photographs: Alvin Ailey Dance Theater (Alicia B. Adams), The Performing Arts Program of the Asia Society (Elaine Goldman), Austrian National Tourist Office (Christine Bosis), Bureau of Indian Affairs, Department of the Interior (Harriet Burgess), Ceylon (Sri Lanka) Tourist Board (Lakshman Ratnapala), Chautauqua Dance Company (Statia Sublette), Chinese Information Service (Simon Peng), Cincinnati Ballet Company (Sally Dunker), Eglevsky Ballet Company (Toby Levy), Lynn Farnol Group (Alice B. Regensburg), Greek Press and Information Service (E. Sotiropoulos), Ghana Tourist Office (Rose-Marie Glouer), Government of India Tourist Office (Jhamandass), Indonesian Consulate General (Achmad Goefron), Israel Government Tourist Office (Lisa Bernstein), Japan National Tourist Organization (Ettie Selinger), Joffrey Ballet (Kenneth P. Marine), Malaysian Tourist Information Centre (Henry S. Lee), P/J's Dance Charisma (Rosemary Parker and Paul Verie), Roseland Ballroom (Ade Kahn), Joyce Trisler Danscompany (Harry Rubenstein), Twyla Tharp Dance Foundation (Debbie Lepsinger), and Dan Wagoner and Dancers (Dan Wagoner and Frank Wicks).

Contents

The World of Dance

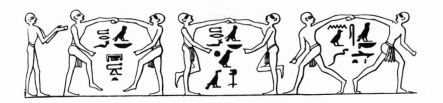

1. Dance Is...

Dance is a group of young couples in a crowded discotheque moving to the electronic beat of a rock group. It is one hundred men on the island of Bali swaying and shaking through the traditional movements of the age-old Monkey Dance.

Dance is a court of nobles and ladies during the reign of Louis XIV of France, dressed in fine robes and powdered wigs, following the dainty steps and graceful turns of the minuet. It is a group of peasants in a tavern roughly and lustily stomping and kicking to the gay music.

Dance is a class of ballet students practicing *pliés* and *relevés*. It is an Apache Indian doing the terrifying Crown Dance to summon forth magical spirits.

Dance is all this—and much, much more. It is the Italian peasants' tarantella, which was used to cure the poisonous bite of the tarantula. It is the modern dancers' free, imaginative movements on a bare stage. It is a gathering of elegantly dressed men and women turning and spinning through the waltz steps at a gay Viennese ball. It is the dancer-actors of the traditional Japanese theater, re-creating their centuries-old dramas. It is a group of Israeli dancers doing the hora, a circle dance whose roots reach way back to the early days of dance history.

Dance is magic. It is a religious or mystical ritual. It is the means to release powerful emotions and to express deep feelings. It is a bridge to out-of-body experiences.

Dance is basic to all people. It is the most widespread and universal of all human activities. Almost all people on earth have dance traditions. Many of these traditions go back thousands of years.

Although all dances are rooted in basic human rhythms and in people's need to express themselves through movement, dances differ from place to place. Mountain people have different dances from people living on the plains. The

Right: Dance is a ballroom filled with dancing couples. *Roseland Ballroom*
Below: Dance is one hundred men on the island of Bali swaying and shaking in the Monkey Dance. *Indonesian Consulate General, New York*

Above: Dance is a class of ballet students perfecting their skills. *Chautauqua Dance Department*

Left: Dance is the free, imaginative movements of modern dance. *Photo: Daniel Eifert; Dan Wagoner and Dancers*

Below: Dance is an Apache Indian executing the terrifying Crown Dance.

Dance is a group of people having fun doing peasant tavern dances that have been passed along for generations. *Austrian National Tourist Office*

dances of people in farming countries are different from the dances of people in industrialized countries. The dances of the Orient are different from the dances of Western countries.

Dances also differ from time to time. Dance styles change as cultures evolve. As people change their ways of life, their dances change too. Old dances are reshaped or fade away. New dances are created. The dances of twentieth-century America, for example, are completely different from the dances of ancient Greece or of medieval Europe.

14

Mountain people tend to have leaping dances, as shown in this photograph from Macedonia.

Dance is magic.

Dance is the stylized movement of traditional Japanese dance-theater.
Japan National Tourist Organization

One way to understand the history of dance is to focus on some of the most important turning points in the development of the art and to associate them with changes taking place in the society of the time. For example, primitive dance changed when tribal organization replaced family organization. Ballet was created during the Renaissance as an expression of the new belief in an ordered, logical world. The waltz replaced the aristocratic minuet as the most popular of all social dances in the mid-eighteenth century, when the

People who live on flat land commonly do chain dances, as shown in this 1900 photograph of the Hopi Indian Snake Dance. *Bureau of Indian Affairs*

This couple wears the rich traditional costume of Malaysia in one type of Oriental dance. *Tourist Development Corporation of Malaysia*

These dancers perform a modern work created by an American choreographer-dancer, Dan Wagoner. *Photo: Daniel Eifert; Dan Wagoner and Dancers*

17

middle class became more powerful and important than the aristocracy. Modern dance reflects the revolutionary spirit of the early years of the twentieth century. The nontouching social dances of the 1960s were part of people's striving to be liberated and free. The popularity of the hustle and other couple dances is a reaction against the disruptions of society in the past and perhaps signals a return to a more caring society.

Throughout history, from primitive days until now, dance has reflected, or mirrored, the times. A selective look at dance through the ages points out its close connection with various chapters of human history. It develops the concept that dance springs from people's basic beliefs and activities. It is a view of dance that was best expressed by the great dance scholar Curt Sachs, who said, ". . . dance in its essence is simply life on a higher level."

2. Primitive Dance

The oldest sources of information about early dance are the cave paintings found in France and Spain, dating back about twenty-five thousand years to Paleolithic times. These paintings not only show how people of that age danced, but also what they ate, the clothes they wore, and their ways of life.

More modern sources of information about ancient dance are the few remaining tribes in Africa, Australia, Asia, and South America that keep up their old cultural traditions. In some of these places it is possible to see dances that have been preserved intact for hundreds, or perhaps even thousands, of years.

The rapid spread of modern technology and culture, however, is destroying the art of these primitive people. Not long ago, for example, a dance scholar visited a remote tribe in the interior of New Guinea to observe their dances. To his amazement, the dance they performed for him resembled the Charleston, a popular jazz dance of the 1920s. He soon learned that the "tribal" dance came from a member who had visited Port Moreseby, a modern city on the coast of New Guinea, where he had seen the Charleston in a movie!

19

Dance scholars learn about primitive dance from 25,000-year-old cave paintings like this one in Cogul, Spain.

In this dance the Australian aborigines imitate the movements of the animals that they hope to capture in the hunt.

Types of Primitive Dance

In the primitive world, above all, dance was magic. The people had little understanding of the laws of nature or of the relationship of cause and effect. To help explain the mysteries around them, they turned to a belief in magic and spirits. And they used dance in the hope that it would help them to influence or control forces and events that they could not comprehend.

One type of primitive magical dance imitates, in a sort of pantomimed way, the objects or situations the dancers are

Knowledge of primitive dance comes from tribes that keep up their ancient cultural traditions. *Ghana Tourist Office*

trying to influence. They mimic the movements and cries of the animals the hunters will be stalking. They act out the battles the warriors will be fighting. The dancers create an image of the animals, people, or situation in order to project their will on them.

Another type of primitive dance is imageless. It makes no effort at imitation. Instead, the dancers strive to reach a state of ecstasy, of exhilaration, of complete abandon, through the dance. They work themselves up into a trancelike frenzy to gain magical power, cure the sick, punish the evil, or guarantee good hunting.

The funeral dance of the Alfuro tribe in the Moluccas, a group of islands off Indonesia, is a good illustration of an image dance. The couples gather in front of the house of the dead person. Facing each other, they join hands and form a bridge. A young child walks over each couple's clasped hands.

To get rid of evil spirits, a fetish priest does an energetic dance that many priests have done before him. *Ghana Tourist Office*

These Pueblo Indians wear buffalo horns and headpieces in this image dance. *Bureau of Indian Affairs*

As the child steps past, the couple moves to the front of the line, extending the bridge farther. The child continues walking in this way until he or she has circled the house eight times. The dance is a concrete image of life renewing itself without end.

The funeral dance of the Dayaks in Borneo, on the other hand, illustrates an imageless dance. It is performed by a single elderly slave woman. She is made to dance around and around a tree in the jungle until she collapses in a stupor. The tree is then chopped down, and the wood is used to make a coffin for the body. A dance of ecstasy, it also portrays renewal and continuity, but without any use of images.

With the passing of time, each type of dance takes on

23

These Pueblo Indians are performing an imageless dance. *Bureau of Indian Affairs*

elements of the other. The image dances become more stylized and abstract. The imageless dances begin to use real, concrete illustrations of the themes of the dances.

This may lead to less interesting and less attractive dances. Or it may lead to blended dances that are better than the dances from which they were derived.

The masked dance, which came in later times, is considered to be a highly successful blended dance. For the image dancers, the mask makes the subject of the dance more intense and real. By wearing a lion's mask, the dancer comes closer to becoming a lion than by just moving and roaring like a lion. Likewise, the imageless dancers create masks that embody their wildest visions of the spiritual and magical world they are trying to enter. The masks help them depart even further from reality.

24

The elaborate mask worn by an Indian dancer intensifies the meaning of the dance. *Government of India Tourist Office, New York*

Dance Accompaniment

The earliest dances probably did not have any beat or melody. The only sounds to accompany these dances were those made by the dancers themselves.

In image dances that imitated the movements of animals, for instance, the dancers produced the cries of the animals as well. The sounds helped the dancers to become more like the animals. It increased the power of the magic. In imageless dances the only sounds were the dancers' emotional cries. They yelled and shouted during vigorous, wild dances, whispered and murmured in the calmer ones.

Many different groups in the world today still use nonmusical sounds in their dances. These sounds have characterized these dances from their very beginnings. In

Above: The whirling dervishes of Turkey say *ooooo,* as they spin and turn in their dances. *Left:* Modern Austrian folk dancers slap their legs in a carry-over from the primitive practice of accompanying dance by slapping parts of the body. *Austrian National Tourist Office*

26

Samoa, and among the Maidu tribe in California, they hum the sound *m-m-m-m*. The whirling dervishes of Turkey say *oooo*. The sleep dancers of Bali use *hooo*. The Indians of northwest Brazil dance to *pooo*. The Buddhists have their *omru*. And the Asturians of Spain shout *hee-yoo-yoo* as they leap through their dances.

In time, rhythmical accompaniment became part of the dance. At first it was just the stamping of the dancers' feet. Then they took to clapping their hands together or slapping their thighs, upper arms, or abdomen.

As dance continued to evolve, noisemakers attached to

These Assiniboine Indians go through the age-old steps of the Mourning Dance, accompanied only by the bells they wear on their ankles. *Bureau of Indian Affairs*

the dancers' bodies added to the beat. The dancers tied strings of shells, stones, or parts of plants around their legs, arms, or neck to add sounds as they moved. From these rhythm "instruments" on the body it was a short step to using separate drums and rattles to accompany the dancers.

The first melodic accompaniments to dance were sung, either by the dancers or by others. Subsequently, melody instruments were introduced. The tunes of the dances were then played on the ancestors of such modern instruments as the flute and the harp.

Since some dances last several hours, the drummers must have great stamina. *Ghana Tourist Office*

Beating half coconut shells together provides the accompaniment for these Malaysian dancers. *Tourist Development Corporation of Malaysia*

Walrus-hide drums are the accompanying instruments for some Eskimo dancers in Alaska. *Bureau of Indian Affairs*

Forms

The family was the basic social unit in the very earliest period of civilization. Many of the oldest dances reflect this social structure. Although these dances were performed by groups, each dancer was independent of the others. They did not touch or have any physical contact. They did not use the same movements or gestures or even keep the same rhythm. Among the Cágaba Indians of Colombia and the Khasis of Indochina, the dancers still do not touch one another.

As the family evolved into tribal units, dance also became more social. Just as people developed closer relationships and became interdependent, the dancers began to touch one another, to use the same steps and movements, and to keep the same rhythm. Sometimes they held hands, locked arms, or placed hands on each other's shoulders or hips. In fact, there are still some children's dances of New Guinea in which the dancers hold on to each other's ears!

From the earliest days, dance took the basic form of the circle. Even chimpanzees have been seen to dance in a circle. For humans, though, the circle dance usually revolved around a central object, a sick person to be cured, an animal to be tamed, a prisoner to be subdued, and so on. The old belief that energy flows from those in the circle to the object in the center or from the center object out to those in the circle persists today.

The circle, which was explored and experienced in dance, is very likely related to the round shape of the first shelters that were built after people moved out of caves. Modern examples are the tribes of American Indians whose dances are largely circular in form, and who traditionally live in round tepees.

Later, the dance took the form of rows or lines of dancers. People associated with these dances, such as the American

In some couple dances that are clearly sexual in meaning, the man's role is to pursue and woo the woman. *Tourist Development Corporation of Malaysia*

Indians of the Northwest, often live in square or rectangular huts.

The first record of a couple dance is found in a French cave painting from the Early Stone Age. The painting shows a masked male dancer following a female dancer. It is believed that men and women were equally important in this early form of dance.

Some primitive couple dances had to do with the stars and planets. In a dance done by the Cora Indians of Mexico, the girl plays the part of earth, while the boy dances the part

The Kandyan Dance from Ceylon, which dates far back in history, is a difficult, strenuous dance, always performed by a line of five or six male dancers. *Director, Ceylon (Sri Lanka) Tourist Board, New York*

of the morning star in a circle around her. In another couple dance from Australia, one dancer represents the light side of the moon; the other, the dark side. As the light dancer grows more powerful and covers more space, the dark partner kneels and finally becomes still.

Other primitive dances are clearly sexual in origin and often relate to fertility. The dance may be a stylized portrayal of the postures and movements of courtship and marriage. It may project love and tenderness, as in a dance from northwest Brazil in which a man moves around the woman with one hand on her shoulder while holding the flute that he plays in the other hand.

Male dancers perform most primitive dances. Only men participate in the hunting, war, and sun dances. They also do most of the animal, rain, and medicine dances, as well as the initiation dances for young men who have come of age. In some societies where dance is exclusively for males, women are forbidden to even watch them.

In male-dominated societies, women have only a small number of their own dances. They do the dances of fertility, harvest, birth, moon, and mourning, as well as the initiation of young girls. As with some of the male dances, members of the opposite sex are forbidden to watch. The punishment for anyone who disobeys may be as severe as being blinded or even put to death.

Movements

Primitive dances include a number of different dance movements, or dance figures, from shaking the head to flexing the toes, from twisting the torso to slapping the thighs. All parts of the dance, though, can be classified as either convulsive or harmonic dancing.

In convulsive dances, the performers shake their bodies until they reach a climax of ecstasy. *Indonesian Consulate General, New York*

Convulsive dances use wild, frenzied movements. The dancers shake and tremble some or all of the muscles of their bodies until they reach a climax of ecstasy and collapse. Harmonic dancing is basically just rhythmic movements. The dancers merely conform to an ongoing beat.

Convulsive dancing is widespread within a few areas in Asia, among the Bantu tribes in Africa, and among some tribes of North American Indians. These people, although scattered over several continents, all have witch-doctor or medicine-man cultures. The hypnotic trance brought on by the convulsive dances is believed to be necessary before they can use their magical healing powers.

Harmonic dances involve either expanded or closed movements. Typical of the expanded movements are the leap, lift, stride, lunge, and skip. The expanded movements are strong. The dancer uses every muscle of the body to fight free of the earth's gravity and to reach up to space.

In leap dances, the object is to jump as high as possible.

The jumping, running movements of this dance from the Punjab area of India classifies it as a dance of expanded movements. *Government of India Tourist Office, New York*

These dances are still found in parts of Europe, India, and Indochina, though they are most widely distributed throughout Africa. Accounts of African dancers describe them as easily soaring several feet into the air.

Cultures where dancers use expanded leap movements are usually found in mountainous or hilly regions. These societies mostly herd cattle or raise animals for food, milk, and furs. In general, they are masculine, patriarchal societies. A patriarchal society is one in which the father is the leader of the family group, and all children become part of the father's family. The dances too are dominated by men. When women are included, they are usually confined to much more reduced movements.

The image dance is most common to these patriarchal societies. Their people tend to be more interested in concrete experiences than in abstract thoughts. They are usually more outgoing and tend to be violent. They frequently are unsteady and erratic in their behavior.

The harmonic dances that use closed movements are usually calmer, more quiet, charming, and graceful. Swinging and swaying are the basic movements. In a way, closed dances resemble warm-up exercises for a class in gymnastics. This group of dances includes sitting dances, in which just the dancer's arms, torso, and head move; belly dances, in which the dancer rotates her pelvis; hand dances, which are so important to East Indian dances; and whirling dances, in which the dancers turn around and around.

Primitive societies that perform closed dances are generally occupied with farming and tilling the soil. They are planters rather than herders or hunters. Since agriculture in primitive societies is largely the responsibility of women, these societies are generally matriarchal. Here the children belong to the mother's family. Her brothers, not the father, are the chief protectors of the family.

35

This seated Malaysian dance uses closed movements. *Tourist Development Corporation of Malaysia*

The imageless dance is characteristic of matriarchal societies. People in matriarchal societies tend to focus more on inner thoughts and feelings than on outside reality. They are generally peaceful, pleasant, and cheerful in their ways. The dances of these societies are performed mostly by the women.

In 1931 the German anthropologist Herbert Baldus visited two adjacent tribes in South America, the Chamacocos and the Kaskihas. The Chamacoco dance was based on expanded movements, including wild leaps, gourd rattling, and loud singing. These people obtained their food by hunting.

Among the Kaskihas, dance was essentially a slow, hesitant walking back and forth movement. The Kaskihas were a farming tribe. The closed form of their dance was typical of primitive people who grew their own food. Although the tribes lived side by side, they had evolved different life-styles and dance-styles.

Choreometrics

During the 1970s, Alan Lomax, a folk-music scholar and collector, began a serious study, called choreometrics, of the elements of dance around the world. He wanted to discover the common forms and movements found in diverse cultures and far-flung parts of the world. Could the various languages of dance be understood as well as spoken languages?

All arm movements, he discovered, could be divided into three basic types: straight line, or one-dimensional, movements; curved, or two-dimensional, movements and spiral, or three-dimensional, movements.

The arm movements of dancers around the world, he found, are associated with the means of production used in their own societies. In less advanced economic systems, where the people use simple wooden tools to scrape, rub, pound, or poke, 70 percent of the arm movements in dance are one dimensional, or straight lined.

In more advanced societies, where people use metal tools, and some build and paddle canoes, the basic work movement is curved in space. The arm movements, in about 80 percent of the dances of these people, are curved, or two dimensional.

And in the most advanced countries, such as China, Japan, and India, where tools and the means of production are highly complex, the arm movements of the dance are likewise complex. In fact, spiral, or three-dimensional, arm movements are used in about 80 percent of the dances of these highly developed cultures.

Lomax and his co-workers spotted two distinct ways in which the torso, that is, the shoulders, trunk, and hips, moves during dance. In one kind of dance, each part of the torso bends, undulates, or moves flexibly and independently. This he called a multi-unit style. In the single-unit style, the torso is held in a stiff, rigid manner and there is little bending.

The torso style, researchers have found, is closely related to climate. Ninety percent of the dances of tropical Africa are multi-unit, as are most of the dances of the blacks in America of African ancestry. The style may also be related to women's work in that society. Most women's tasks in the tropical areas of the world involve grinding grains, weaving, and other jobs that require undulating body movements.

The single-unit torso dance predominates in the cold areas of the world and among people who originally came from these areas. Eskimos, North and South American Indians, as well as people in lands around the Pacific, all perform a similar style of dance. These people are descended from ancestors who once lived in the cold climate of Siberia. Similarly, 90 percent of European dance is single unit, because most of today's Europeans originated in the northern part of the Continent. The Irish jig is a good example of a single-unit dance whose beauty depends on keeping the upper body and head stiff and unmoving while going through complex steps with the feet.

In their search for overall patterns in dance, the choreometricians have made some interesting discoveries concern-

The members of the Masai tribe in Kenya are famous for their leap dances.

ing arm movements and torso style. European dance, they learned, is essentially single unit and two dimensional. Dance in Africa and around the Pacific Ocean is multi-unit and two dimensional. The Orient is largely single unit, with three-dimensional arm movements, while in India and Southeast Asia the pattern is mostly multi-unit with three-dimensional arm movements.

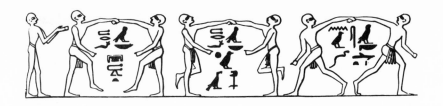

3. Dances of the Ancient Egyptians and Hebrews

Egypt

The dawn of a new era in the cultural history of the world took place some seven thousand years ago, around the year 5000 B.C. Some people along the fertile banks of the Nile River in Northeast Africa were the first to change from the old ways of hunting and gathering food to farming.

Farming marks the break with primitive society and the beginning of a social system. With a social system, civilization and culture were able to develop. By 4000 B.C. these people were unified into the state of Egypt under the rule of the pharaoh.

Until about 1500 B.C., the dances of the ancient Egyptians were stiff, formal, and restrained. The movements of the dancers were highly angular; their gestures were extremely stylized. Their postures and positions looked very similar to those seen on paintings that have come down to us from that period.

In time, social structures developed in the new country. The primitive magical practices grew into organized religious observances. A class of priests arose and temples were built.

This ancient drawing shows two Egyptian male dancers advancing, turning each other around, and withdrawing.

Special religious dances were performed in the temples and became an important part of the worship.

Dancing was also an important part of the celebrations that surrounded the worship of the Egyptian's favorite gods, Osiris and Isis. According to legend, Osiris was married to Isis, his sister. An enemy, Set, killed him, laid him in a coffin, and flung him into the Nile. Isis began to search for his body, but Set found it first and cut it into fourteen parts, scattering the pieces throughout the land. Isis, though, was able to find them. The Sun God took pity on Isis and helped her to resurrect Osiris.

The celebration honoring Osiris, the god of vegetation, fertility, and the life-giving Nile River, took place in midsummer when the corn was ripening. A bas-relief in the Louvre from the time of Pharaoh Sesostris III, around 1850 B.C., shows that festivals to Osiris were already being celebrated. Often the high priest himself would enact the part of Osiris in a drama that told the story of the god's resurrection.

The festival of Isis, who shed tears for Osiris, was held in June as the Nile waters started to rise. These festivals were important because the waters of the Nile made agriculture possible. The well-being of the people depended on the river's ebb and flow. If the waters became too high or flowed too strongly, the crops were destroyed and there was famine in the land. If the waters did not rise high enough to fill the irrigation canals, there was drought and, again, famine. Worship of these gods, it was hoped, would cause the Nile to rise to a level that would ensure good harvests.

The celebrations were mostly held in two cities, Abydos, where Isis found Osiris' head, and in Busiris, where she found his spine. It was celebrated by the temple priests, as well as by the people. Many of the dancers wore either masks or elaborate head ornaments. Some of the masks showed a face with a closed mouth. This was to symbolize the fact that the festival told the legend of Osiris through dance and mime, not through speech.

During the eighteen-day festival, the early parts of the Osiris legend were told through dance: the story of his birth, the games he played as a child, his love for his sister. Then, the most important parts were reenacted: his struggle with Set, the tragedy of his death and dismemberment, the search for his body, the joy of discovery, and the exultation of his resurrection.

Apart from the Osiris cult, there were other magical dance festivals. One of the most popular, a carry-over of the primitive fertility rites, was a ceremony to honor the bull, Apis.

Each year a healthy, black bull was carefully selected by the priests. The bull had to have white triangles on his forehead and right flank, the image of an eagle formed by the hairs on his back, and under his tongue there had to be a lump in the shape of a scarab beetle.

For four months the bull was kept in a special stable, fed only milk, and was tended by forty nude virgins. Just before the festival, the bull was taken on a golden barge to the city of Memphis, where the people greeted him with songs and dances. From Memphis, he was transported to Apeum, where the priests performed their secret dances before the animal. Finally, the bull was sacrificed.

A group of astronomer-priests performed the secret Dance of the Stars. Around the altar, which represented the sun, they moved from east to west, like the planets. As they slowly rotated around the sun, they made the various signs of the zodiac with their hands. After completing the circle, the priests froze in their positions to symbolize the permanency of the earth amidst the many changes in nature.

Carvings and paintings from ancient Egypt show that there was usually some sort of accompaniment to the dance. In a few representations either the dancer or an observer is clapping hands to provide a rhythmic beat. Sometimes musicians playing instruments or women singing a musical accompaniment are shown.

From the earliest days of Egyptian civilization until its decline around 525 B.C., dance was part of religious rituals.

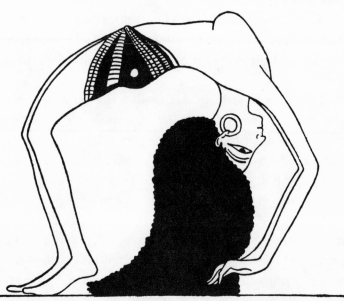

This drawing, made from a bas-relief, shows a woman in the famous bridge position of Egyptian dance.

The peasants and lower classes also danced at many of the festivals and celebrations. But the upper classes of Egypt, the nobles and rulers who managed the estates and collected the taxes, seldom danced themselves. They hired professional dancers or trained slaves to perform for them. These dancing girls entertained them at parties, celebrations, funerals, banquets, and on other occasions.

The trained dancers included acrobatics in their movements. Some dancers juggled objects, such as wine goblets, as they danced and moved like belly dancers. One painting shows a male dancer throwing a female dancer to another male. Their dances were quite different from those done in the temples.

Some scholars believe that ballet, which developed much, much later, derived from these early Egyptian dances. A 1600 B.C. carving from Beni Hasan shows a *pirouette*, a turn on one foot. A similar carving shows an *entrechat*, a leap with repeated leg crosses in midair.

Two bas-reliefs of the time show women doing the split. A much more frequent picture, though, shows the position called the bridge. The dancer's hands and feet are on the ground, back arched, abdomen up. This position had two meanings for the ancient Egyptians. The bridge represented the arch of the sky over the earth. It also showed the wind blowing back the reed grass that grows along the Nile. The bridge position was used so often that it became an ideogram, a symbol that represented acrobatic dance.

The Old Kingdom, from 3400 to about 2475 B.C., and the Middle Kingdom, until 1580 B.C., were the periods of the great pyramid and temple builders in Egypt. The pharaohs and nobles believed they would live beyond death. They were buried in the pyramids and temples with pots of food, furniture, tools, jewels, and charms to sustain and protect them in the next world.

The pyramids symbolize a culture that sought permanence and stability and resisted death, change, and decay. The perfect abstract geometrical shape of these tombs, built for all eternity, are representations in stone of the goals of the Egyptians. They bespeak a world of absolutes, where every person had a specific role in society, without any concern for personal differences or individual growth and development.

The walls of these tombs are covered with pictures that now serve as a guide to the culture of the time. From them we learn that the Egyptians danced for their gods and for the pleasure of the nobles. The hieroglyphic writings name the dance steps that were done.

Great changes took place during the New Kingdom, beginning around 1580 B.C. By this time Egypt had become a vast, powerful kingdom, and Egyptian armies had captured people in distant lands and brought some back to Egypt as prisoners. Among them were the *bayaderes*, the temple dancers from India, who were to have a major impact on Egyptian dance.

Along with the new influences from abroad came a relaxation and a general loosening of Egyptian thought and ideas. The paintings show a new liveliness and spirit of freedom, with more individualism and greater human warmth. The figures are more relaxed and even tender with one another. They are shown performing such ordinary tasks as washing and dressing.

Dance, too, reflected this change of outlook. While in the past it had been hard and linear, it now became softer and the movements more flowing. Under the influence of the bayaderes, the strong, stiff masculine movements of the older Egyptian style gave way to a more sinuous, feminine style of dance.

But this period of Egyptian life did not last very long. After a while, the people went back to their old ways.

Female dancers in this tomb painting from about 1400 B.C. are portrayed in the softer, more flowing movements of the New Kingdom.

Gradually the stiff, angular, geometric movements of the past took over the freer, more intimate dances that had typified the New Kingdom. A belief in many gods replaced the worship of a single god. After the period of peace, there was a return to warfare and annexation of new territories. The country prospered for a while. But then a series of foreign invaders overran the land of Egypt. The great civilization entered a decline from which it never fully recovered.

In Egypt, for the first time in world history, dance played an important part in the culture of a civilization. Though it was dedicated to worshipping gods and entertaining nobles, the ideas and art of Egyptian dance outlasted the collapse of the Egyptian civilization and spread from there to much of the Western world.

47

This drawing from an early Christian manuscript is entitled "Mary and the Hebrew Maidens Dancing."

Hebrews

Some of the oldest and best descriptions of dancing among the Hebrew people are found in the Bible. The first dance is mentioned in the Book of Exodus 15:20. The Israelites are fleeing from their slavery in Egypt. They have just safely crossed the Red Sea and are celebrating their deliverance from the pursuing Egyptian soldiers. The Bible describes one part of the celebration: "And Miriam the prophetess, the sister of Aaron, took a timbrel [a tambourine] in her hand; and all the women went out after her with timbrels and with dances."

Later, when Moses was on Mount Sinai receiving the Ten Commandments, he learned that the Israelites had built a Golden Calf, which they were worshipping. Moses descended from the mountain, "And it came to pass, as soon as he came nigh unto the camp, that he saw the calf, and the dancing . . ." (Exodus 32:19).

In a rage, Moses flung down the tablets on which the Ten Commandments were written, completely smashing them. "And he took the calf which they had made, and burnt *it* in the fire . . ." (Exodus 32:20).

Dance scholars believe that the dance around the Golden Calf was a convulsive circle dance. It was probably the same as many primitive convulsive dances that are part of the dance traditions of so many ancient people.

Most of the dances described in the Bible are to celebrate

One of the first dances described in the Bible is Miriam's dance of celebration after crossing the Red Sea.

or commemorate important religious or historical moments or day-to-day events. One vivid account describes the two lines of dancers at the dedication of the walls of Jerusalem during the time of the prophets Ezra and Nehemiah. It tells of other dancers on the same occasion who threw flaming torches into the air and caught them.

One of the most joyous Hebrew holidays is the Feast of Tabernacles. It is traditionally celebrated with processions in which participants carry branches with lemons attached to them. In biblical times, men of the community, chosen for their good deeds and high scholarship, carried the torches and danced around the altar. One scholar believes that these wild, joyous dances brought the Hebrew prophets to a state of ecstasy in which they proclaimed the message of Jehovah and revealed His will to the people.

For the most part, dances mentioned in the Bible were freely improvised. There were no set steps, movements, or forms. They sprang spontaneously from the emotions of the dancers and the immediate purposes and circumstances of the dance. Many of the dances took place in the temple, but everyone danced, not just the priests. There was, though, a careful separation of men and women. In all cases, a leader set the general tone and direction for the dance gestures.

Perhaps the greatest dance leader mentioned in the Bible is King David, who ruled from about 1000 to 970 B.C. In the second book of Samuel 6:14, it says: "And David danced before the Lord with all *his* might." His dance is further described (6:16) as a wild dance, with many violent leaps and jumps, probably in a circle form.

Most joyous family events, such as marriages and births, were celebrated by dance. Harvest, too, was a reason to dance, as was courting. In the book of Judges 21:21, there is an account of the vineyard festival at Shiloh: "And see, and, behold, if the daughters of Shiloh come out to dance in

50

A section of an eleventh-century mosaic in Venice shows Salome dancing with the head of John the Baptist.

dances, then come ye out of the vineyards, and catch you every man his wife of the daughters of Shiloh."

Best known of all dances described in the Bible is probably Salome's dance before King Herod (Matthew 14:6). Salome, no ordinary woman, in this legend performs a solo dance, customarily done only in private. It is now believed that the part of the story that deals with Salome's wearing and removing seven veils was added long after the biblical period.

For the religious, the most significant dance is the one prophesied by the ancient sage Rabbi Eleazar: "Someday the Holy One, blessed be He, will give a dance for the righteous, and He will sit among them in the Garden of Eden, and each one will point his finger at Him, saying as it is written, 'Lo, this is our God; we have waited for Him and He will save us.' "

Salome is dancing before Herod in this drawing by an unknown fourteenth-century artist.

Some of the dances done today in modern Israel, such as this joyous Hasidic one, may include remnants of the dances of the ancient Hebrews. *Israel Government Tourist Office*

Since Jews are forbidden by law to represent the human form in art, there are no picture records of ancient Hebrew dances. From the Bible we know of circle dances, processional dances, and hopping, stamping dances. Some of the dances done today in modern Israel at traditional feasts and weddings use chants and stamping steps that may date back to the dances of thousands of years ago.

4. Dances of the Ancient Greeks and Romans

The Greeks

The ancient Greeks borrowed many of their dance forms, as well as their moral and religious ideas, from the Egyptians and from peoples of other lands. But the most important influence was probably the ancient Cretan, or Minoan, culture, which lasted from about 3400 to 1200 B.C.

Crete is an island in the Mediterranean that lies between Egypt and Greece. During the early years of the Cretan civilization, sailors and travelers from Egypt brought elements of Egyptian culture to Crete. Cretans adapted the abstract, geometrical art of Egypt. They made it freer and more elegant, with curves and ornaments. Cretan cultural development peaked around 1600 B.C. During the next few centuries, the Cretan cities were overrun by the Greeks. The Greeks chose the most attractive aspects of Cretan art and brought them to the Greek mainland.

The Greeks particularly liked the dance of the Cretans. They brought many of Crete's finest dancers to Greece. In the seventh century B.C. the famous Cretan musician Thaletas was brought to Sparta to fight the plague with

Cretan dances and songs. The several types of Cretan dance that were brought to the mainland were molded and shaped by the Greek way of thinking. They became the foundation of later Greek dance.

There is one particular dance legend of Crete that influenced dance in Greece. According to the legend, the god Zeus was born to Kronos and Rhea. Rhea, afraid that Kronos would kill and eat the child, fled to Crete with the infant. In an early Cretan magical dance, springing from the primitive ritual of frightening away evil spirits, young men who have just reached maturity, Kouretes, dance wildly around the baby. They beat swords against shields as they shout and leap about, so that Kronos will not hear the baby's cries.

In Greece the dance was performed by a single Kouros, a dance leader, and a chorus. The theme is similar to the Osiris legend in Egypt. It is the story of death and resurrection that appears in the beliefs of people all over the world. The dancer enacted the story of the infant who is protected by the armed Kouretes. But the child is killed and dismembered by a tribe of giants. Later, the child comes back to life in a concluding resurrection episode.

Eventually the dance became an imitative weapon dance known as the *pyrrhiche,* in which the performers went through stylized attack and defense fighting motions. The accompaniment was either the singing of the dancers, chords struck on a harp, or a melody played on a flute.

The pyrrhiche was taught to Greek youngsters starting at the age of five. The movements and steps were athletic. The participants marched, charged, retreated, and defended in a stylized way. In fact, the movements of the pyrrhiche dance and actual combat were so similar that often the best dancers were considered the best warriors.

The early Greeks added elements of exercise or calisthenics to the magical and imitative aspects of Cretan dance. They held that dance was an excellent way to improve the body and to bring about a greater harmony between mind and body. In keeping with their basic philosophy that civilization needed the free and full participation of all citizens in the city, everyone danced, not just priests or professionals.

All the gestures of Greek dance were organized and codified as the *cheironomia*. Originally, the cheironomia was a series of static poses, related to positions taken in combat. In time, cheironomia came to mean rhythmical movements of the hands. Hundreds have been recorded, each one with its own specific meaning, for example, a hand on the head

More than two thousand years ago, the ancient Greeks made dance more athletic. This modern photo shows the Official Greek Guards doing the Kalamatianos, a vigorous folk dance that carries on the old tradition. *Greek Press and Information Service*

This painting from ancient Greece shows a dancing maiden serving wine at a banquet.

shows grief, reaching up with the hands is prayer, a thrust forward is a sword stroke, and so on. As time went on, the cheironomia became more like pantomime.

The original Greek dances were all choral, or group, dances. In fact, the very word *choral* probably comes from the Greek word *choreia*, which stems from the word *chara*, or joy. Among the many choral dances were the *paeans* to Apollo, the god of healing. The paeans were lively dances in which everyone sang and danced. The *hyporchemata*, also dedicated to Apollo, were danced by a chorus of dancers who mimed the text as it was being sung. The *gymnopedia*, danced by a chorus of men, youths, and naked boys, was dedicated to the memory of those slain at the important battle of Thermopylae. And the *emmeleia* was a slow, sedate

57

The male figure on the left plays the flute and dances, while the *maenad*, in leopard-skin costume, plays the clappers as she dances.

dance performed mostly by women, usually in procession to a shrine, where it was followed by a circle dance around the shrine itself.

Most of the choral dances were restrained and orderly. They reflected the Greek's striving for perfection and sense of balance and harmony. The Greek mind tried to reduce the complex to simple elements, to replace tension with relaxation, and to dissipate heated passions with logic and rational thought.

Besides these tightly controlled dances, there were the wild, orgiastic dances dedicated to Dionysus, the god of grapes and all green plants. With head thrown back, torso twisted, and arms wildly thrashing about, the dancers dizzily turned and leapt until they reached a state of ecstasy, followed by collapse and release.

The men dancing for Dionysus played the parts of satyrs, mythical beings that are part men and part beasts. They wore goatskins and horned masks. Some wore beards and tails as well. Their wild, drunken steps were accompanied by pipes and rattles. The women were called *maenads,* or mad women. They were said to be possessed by various gods and spirits. In the course of their dances, they left their homes, stamping and whirling, and climbed the snow-covered mountains. Their outdoor dances of joy and abandon often lasted several days and nights.

One of the Dionysian rites, the springtime *dithyramb,* led

The satyrs and maenads can be seen here celebrating a Dionysian rite.

to the development of Greek drama, both tragedy and comedy. The dance, originally performed by fifty circling garlanded dancers, tells of the birth of Dionysus, his tests of fire and water, and his rebirth. Along with the dancing, there was singing and spoken parts.

In one singing dance, the leading performer wore a goat

The dances dedicated to Dionysus were wild and gay, as shown in this vase painting from the fourth century B.C.

mask. The Greek word for goat song is *tragodia*, which led to the English word *tragedy*. The entire group of people who sang and danced in the procession was called a *komos*, from which is derived the English word *comedy*. In both Greek tragedy and comedy, dance was used with music and poetry for a total theatrical experience. In fact, dance and poetry were so close that each poetic meter is described as a foot, and two feet is known as a stepping.

Dancers were always highly regarded in Greece. Lucian wrote, "The most noble and greatest personages in every city are the dancers. . . ." The Greek dancers performed for all celebrations, for worship, for drama, for everyday events, and for war. But as Greek civilization went into decline, about 336 B.C., the earlier choral dances were replaced almost entirely by more violent dramatic dances. The themes of these late Greek dances were death, war, pain, and disease.

All that we know of the dance steps and movements of the ancient Greeks has been gleaned from writings and from a number of faded paintings and worn sculpture from that time. But these records of classical dance in Greece were enough to inspire the beginnings of ballet some two thousand years later.

Rome

Ancient Rome traces its origins back to about 700 B.C. By the year 146 B.C. the Romans were at the height of their power. They had conquered Greece and made it into a Roman province. Just as the Greeks borrowed from the Cretans, the Romans adapted many aspects of Greek culture. Their early dances, for example, were closely modeled on Greek choral dances.

A group of these Roman dances was called *salii*. One of

61

them, most like a Greek dance, was the Troy Dance, also called Ariadne's Dance. It was performed around a minotaur, a mythological creature with a man's body and a bull's head.

The *tripudium* was a dance of the priests of Mars, who was the god of vegetation before he became the god of war. The priests were dressed in tall conical caps and embroidered tunics. Each one carried a spear in his right hand and a shield in his left. Three was the magic number for this dance. The dance was part of a three-day celebration, it used a three-step pattern, and it was repeated three times. The dancers beat with their swords on the shields as they marched around in circles, leading animals, such as pigs, rams, or bulls, that were to be sacrificed to the god Mars.

The *Saturnalia*, perhaps the best known of the *salii* dances, began on December 17 and lasted one week. Presumably it was started by Romulus at the time of the winter solstice. It signaled a time for masters and slaves to join together in gay drinking, dancing, and singing festivities. Part of the celebration was the exchange of gifts, usually candles and dolls, the latter a remnant of human sacrificial rites. These traditional practices, in time, became part of the Christian celebration of Christmas.

The usual accompaniment for the salii dances was the rhythmic beating of short swords against metal shields. Other Roman dances were accompanied either by the flute, by various types of percussion instruments, or often by the singing of young boys.

Dance declined during the middle period of the Roman civilization, from about 264 until 133 B.C. Roman dancers, as well as poets, musicians, and actors, once respected members of society, were now demeaned and debased. While the Romans still enjoyed watching dance as a spectacle, they now considered it an activity to be performed by slaves and foreigners, not Romans. Dancing slaves were bought and sold

These Roman maidens from the first century B.C. show the Greek influence in their dancing positions.

and rented out for entertainments. They were flogged if they did not please. A writer of the time, Sallust, commenting on a woman's dancing wrote: "She played and danced more gracefully than a respectable woman should."

Rome's greatest contribution to world dance came with the development of pantomime during the final period of its civilization, the Empire period (27 B.C. to A.D. 180). The word

63

A mosaic from Pompeii shows masked dancers performing in a Roman theatrical work.

pantomime comes from the Greek words *pantos,* "all," and *mimeomai,* "to imitate or counterfeit." Pantomime is a dramatic art that uses gesture and movement, not words, to express its meaning.

Why did mimicry, which had always been part of dance, flower during the period of the Roman Empire?

As a result of Roman conquests, people from as far away as present-day England and Scotland, Syria, Greece, Algeria, Spain, Germany, and Egypt were brought together in ancient Rome. These people spoke many different languages. They did not understand the Roman's Latin. Therefore, they could not enjoy spoken drama. Also, the voices of the performers could never be heard above the noise of the large crowds that filled the theaters.

Pantomime is the universal language of the dramatic arts. The exaggerated, bigger-than-life movements and gestures of the pantomimist could easily be seen and understood in the vast Roman amphitheaters where dramatic spectacles were performed.

Pylades and Bathyllus are credited with the invention of Roman pantomime, around 22 B.C. In the early form of pantomime, an actor first summarized the story in words. Then a solo performer retold the story using stylized gestures and movements, often to the accompaniment of a flute and drum. The pantomimist wore a closed-mouth mask to symbolize a story told without words. The full cloak that covered his body was flung about, folded, tied, and draped in many different ways to help tell the tale. The highest praise of pantomime, according to an account of the day, was made by the cynical Demetrius after a performance of the leading pantomimist of Nero's reign. "Man," he shrieked, "this is not seeing, but hearing and seeing, both: 'tis as if your hands were tongues!"

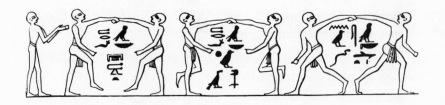

5. Dances of the Orient

India

According to traditional Indian belief, the god Siva created the universe. Then he started to dance, setting the world into motion. Hindu statues of this god usually show him with a leg raised in a dance step and with his many arms in various gestures that symbolize his power to destroy and re-create the universe.

The Hindu dances that are performed today have changed little from the early primitive dances. They derive from the method of Bharata, a sage who lived around the year 500 B.C. His teachings, at first passed down from teacher to student and then written down almost one thousand years later, are believed by the Hindus to be of divine inspiration.

Bharata's sacred textbook on the art of dance is known as the *Natya Sastra*, or *Science of Dancing*. It contains a complete dance system with very detailed instructions on how to use the many different parts of the body, including nine gestures for the head, eight glances of the eye, six movements for the eyebrows, and more than four thousand gestures of the hands. Each movement and gesture imitates

Classical Indian dance includes nine head gestures, eight glances of the eye, six movements for the eyebrows, and more than four thousand hand gestures. *Government of India Tourist Office, New York*

This tenth-century bronze statue shows the grace and beauty of the *devadasis*, the sacred Indian temple dancers. *Metropolitan Museum of Art*

either some actual object—a fish in water, a bird on the wing, or an abstract mood, such as love, hate, fear, surprise.

From the beginning, the Hindu dances have been tied in closely with the Hindu religion. They are usually inseparable from *padanes*, or religious songs. Temple dancers were called *devadasis*, or slaves of the god. They devoted their lives to the dance. They considered their work an act of religious devotion, not for the entertainment or amusement of others. The dancer's steps, as well as the singer's words, were improvised within or around a set pattern.

More than two thousand years ago four major schools of

The style of dance in southeast India is the *Bharatya Natyam,* best known for the skillful use of *mudras,* or hand gestures. *Government of India Tourist Office, New York*

Indian dance began to develop from the early Hindu dance. Each has its own version of the gestures and movements of the *Natya Sastra*.

The style practiced in southeast India is the *Bharatya Natyam* school of gestures. These are the dances most often shown in temple sculptures. They were performed at one time only by devadasis. They are now performed by girls who are carefully trained from a very early age. The dances express the nine *rasas*, or emotions, of dance. These are heroism, fear, love, humor, fury, pathos, wonder, digust, and tranquillity. The dancers project the rasas through the use of their body, eyes, facial expression, neck, hands, and especially vigorous foot movements. Their skillful use of hand gestures, or *mudras*, in portraying people, objects, or feelings is particularly well known.

The *Kathakali* style is centered in southwest India. The dance here is very strong and energetic and is sometimes referred to as danced drama. Dressed in billowing costumes and wearing heavy makeup, the dancers use mime to enact the lives of gods and demons. Very effective lighting and loud drumming contribute to the mood of mystery and excitement. Kathakali dancers have mudras for every word in a sentence, even for the punctuation marks!

From Manipur, in northeast India, come the soft, graceful *Manipuri* dances. Through gentle turns and swaying movements, dotted by vigorous steps and acrobatic leaps, the dancers retell the legends of Krishna, one of the most important of the Hindu gods. Often, the entire village joins in the performances of Manipuri dances.

The *Kathak* dance style is from the northwest part of India. This is the only style to show a strong Moslem influence. It probably dates from the invasion of India by Moslem conquerors. Although these dances also tell the legends of the gods, they are depicted in a secular court style,

Above: The southwest Indian style of dance is *Kathakali,* a storytelling kind of dance, performed with strong, energetic movements. *Government of India Tourist Office, New York*

Left: The *Kathak* dance style centered in northwest India is a secular style, very much influenced by the Moslems. *Government of India Tourist Office, New York*

rather than as religious temple dances, since it is forbidden to represent god in the Moslem religion. Moslems, unlike the Hindus, look on dancing as entertainment. The tapping of the feet and the beating of the drums grows faster and louder, while the arms continue the graceful movements seen in Kathak dances but not in any of the other Hindu styles. (Incidentally, Spanish dancing, also strongly influenced by the Moslems, shows this same contrast of powerful foot stamping with lyrical arm movements.)

Indian dancing spread north by overland trade routes. Among the Indians heading north were Buddhist priests from northern India who brought Indian ways into Tibet and then east into China, Korea, and Japan. By sea, the Indians brought their dancing as well as their goods to eastern Asia.

China

In China, the basic character of Indian dance was greatly changed by the Chinese way of life. The Chinese people were more concerned with human activities than with the worship of a deity. Instead of treating dance as the prime art, as in India, the Chinese combined Indian dance with music, mime, and drama to create a uniquely Chinese theatrical form.

Chinese theater, a far cry from Indian dancing, became an early form of opera. Instead of telling the stories of the gods, the dances tell of emperors who ruled long ago, of wars and battles, and of the affairs of men. Instead of complicated hand gestures, the Chinese used simple imitative gestures. And instead of the simple musical accompaniment of Indian dance, the Chinese used an entire orchestra, with a variety of instruments.

The actors in today's performances of the old Chinese

71

dance dramas paint their faces, much like the performers in the ancient Kathakali plays. The makeup shows the type of character that they represent. Much of the Chinese dance involves eleven basic positions, such as standing, kneeling, stooping, and so on. The stately, static dance consists largely of changing from one position to another. To the Chinese, Western dance by comparison appears to be full of "foolish jumping" and "endless turning." Confucius, the great Chinese philosopher who lived about twenty-five hundred years ago, said that dance should be mild and delicate, never violent or passionate.

Dancer Hung-Yen Hu wears the costume and makeup of a modest young lady of good breeding. *Performing Arts Program of the Asia Society*

Right: The Cup Dance is an ancient Chinese folk dance. The position shown resembles that of a Spanish flamenco dancer. *Chinese Information Service*

Below: Chinese dance is stately and static. In the Sword Dance the sword is a symbol of beauty, not a weapon. *Chinese Information Service*

The *Gagaku* is an old Japanese dance designed to be performed at the Royal Court with masked dancers. *Japan National Tourist Organization*

Japan

Dance dramas came to Japan from China about two thousand years ago. The most ancient Japanese dance, the *Bugaku,* is a slow, dignified dance that was done almost exclusively in the Royal Court for the lords and nobles. Other related dances are the masked *Gagaku,* the acrobatic *Dengaku,* and the mimed *Sarugaku.*

Later, Japanese drama, which merged dance steps and music, appeared. About five hundred years ago the courtly *noh* plays were first performed. In these dramatic presentations the performers, wearing wooden masks, skillfully performed their dance dramas to an orchestral accompaniment. Two hundred years later, *kabuki* plays came into being. These were more elaborate and more dramatic entertainments. The performers painted masks on their faces and included graceful dances and clever mime in the drama.

Over the last centuries, the dances of Eastern lands have

74

In the Japanese *noh* dance-dramas, the performers wear wooden masks.
Japan National Tourist Organization

The most elaborate and dramatic Japanese dance works are the *Kabuki*
plays. *Japan National Tourist Organization*

undergone much less change than the dances of the Western world. When the dancers of India, China, Japan, and the other Asian countries learn to dance, they attempt to re-create the centuries-old dance as exactly and as perfectly as they can, without any thought of change. European and American dancers, on the other hand, take apart the separate elements handed down to them in their dance tradition and reorder and recombine them into new patterns and forms.

The actual steps and movements of Oriental dance are also different from the more familiar Western dances. The movements of Oriental dance are more earth-bound. The dancers do not strive to break free of gravity or to achieve lightness and elevation. The dancers treat every part of the body separately, instead of as a single unit.

Oriental dancers, such as these Javanese girls doing a bow-and-arrow dance, try to perform the old dances as faithfully as they can. *Indonesian Consulate General, New York*

Right: Oriental dancers are usually earth-bound, like this dancer from Ceylon. *Director, Ceylon (Sri Lanka) Tourist Board, New York*

Below: There is much posing and posturing in Oriental dance and the use of many different props. *Indonesian Consulate General, New York*

Oriental dances may seem static and subdued to Westerners. There is much posing and posturing and the use of such props as fans, swords, and scarves. The heavily costumed actors use mime and music, along with dance, to retell the old tales taken from history. But Easterners who are accustomed to these movements and costumes appreciate the grace and skill of the performers.

This dancer from the island of Timor shows both the static quality and the rich costuming of Oriental dance. *Indonesian Consulate General, New York*

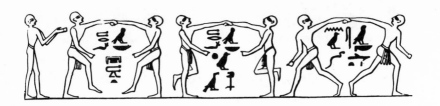

6. Dances of the Dark and Middle Ages

After the Fall of Rome

During the fifth century A.D., tribes from northern Europe, the Goths, Huns, Anglo-Saxons, Vandals, and others, overran the lands under Roman control. The Romans called them barbarians or uncivilized people. They were pagans, superstitious and fierce in their appearance and behavior.

During the early years of their conquest of western Europe, from about A.D. 500 to 800, civilization fell to a low point. Education and culture were almost forgotten. Schools disappeared. Little remained of Greek and Roman art, knowledge, or the principles of law and order. The period is sometimes described as the Dark Ages.

The dances of these pagan people were wild and ritualistic. They were primitive in theme, form, and style. Bishop Caesarius of Arles wrote an account of a Goth celebration around the year 500. It describes a banquet with an animal sacrifice, followed by a wild, frenzied dance accompanied by sexually suggestive and obscene songs.

The Christian church was in the early stages of its development. The church leaders wanted to make Christians of the barbarians. They wanted to overcome the pagan barbarian influences. Many of the church fathers were against dancing. An early Christian called dance "a lascivious madness" and "the devil's business."

Yet the first Christians did not ban dancing. They realized that they could never completely overcome the pagan rites. They hoped that in time, as the ideas of Christianity spread, the dances would lose their magical meaning and significance.

The fact is that as the Christian faith spread among the people, the popular pagan dances became adapted to the purposes of the church. Some symbolic dancing was allowed in churches. A few of these ancient dance rituals have survived to our own day. The Mardi Gras Parade in New Orleans and other cities before Lent is part of a tradition of church dance that dates back to the Dark Ages. There are also dances from this period that are still performed in the Cathedral of Toledo in Spain and in church processions in Sicily, Italy, and Nice, France.

Despite the spreading influence of the church and the pressures on people to adopt the Christian faith, dance during the Dark Ages was mostly a continuation of primitive dance. Fertility was still the central theme. The most important dance festivals were held on the first of May, at midsummer, at weddings, and at funerals. There were circle dances for rain, Maypole and mask dances, sex and sword dances. May fairs, June brides, Halloween pranks, and Christmas carols are modern versions of these pagan rituals.

Although many of the old ways remained, dances based on human and animal sacrifice disappeared. Also, there were fewer animal dances as the invaders from the north changed from hunters to planters and tillers of the soil.

This etching by Israhel Van Meckenem shows one form of dancing madness.

Dansomania

During the ninth century, Europe entered a new period, the Middle Ages. The predominant form of government was feudalism. Dukes, counts, and princes each owned vast tracts of land. They also owned the serfs or peasants who worked the land.

The early years of the Middle Ages were a time of great fear. The church leaders spoke of "Judgment Day," the day of reckoning that would come in the year 1000. Disease was widespread, and large numbers of people died very young.

Those who did not die of disease perished in wars between the lords defending their large fiefs. Drought and floods also caused starvation, which led to many deaths.

It is not surprising, therefore, that out of these troubled times arose a new kind of dancing. Generally, these were wild, hysterical, frenzied dances. The dancers would twirl and hop for hours, or sometimes days, until they collapsed in trancelike states, often foaming at the mouth. The entire phenomenon came to be known as dansomania, or dancing madness.

There are few authentic accounts of dansomania. One written by Giraldus Cambrensis describes boys and girls singing and dancing around a graveyard. Then, suddenly, one falls to the ground as if in a trance, only to rise a short while

In 1493, Hartmann Schedel made this fanciful drawing of a *dance macabre.*

later in a frenzy of movement. When the dance was over, the performers had no recollection of what had happened.

There are many legends and fanciful tales of dansomania. According to one account, for instance, eighteen young men and fifteen young girls started dancing in the graveyard of a church in Paris on Christmas eve, 1013. The priest urged them either to enter the church and take part in the mass or leave. They refused, whereupon the priest put a curse on them: They would sing and dance without stop for an entire year. When they finally stopped at the end of the year, the story goes, three of the girls had died. Since these dances took place mostly in church graveyards, they came to be known as *danse macabre*, from the Arabic *maqbir*, which means tombs or graves.

The year 1000 passed without the world coming to an end, and some of the fear subsided. There was peace and security and improved economic conditions during the eleventh and twelfth centuries. But in the 1300s people once again became discontented. Industry and trade fell off. Peasants revolted against their lords. Workmen fought the merchants who kept them poor. And the Black Death, one of the worst epidemics of all time, swept across Europe, killing about one fourth of the people.

As these disasters struck, the dance madness of the tenth century flared up again. Danse macabre reached a new peak during the time of the Black Death.

The danse macabre helped people deal with their fear of death and of the plague. In an account of danse macabre in Hungary, one of the dancers lies on the ground with a cloth over his face. The bagpipes play a slow, funereal tune. The other dancers slowly circle the single dancer, singing and wailing their grief. Finally they stand him up and try to make the limp form come to life and dance by moving his legs and body.

83

In another version of this dance, all the girls kiss the mock corpse and bring it back to life. Both versions of the dance enact the themes of death and rebirth, so important to primitive thinking. (Since this dance was used when the plague was threatening a town, it has been suggested that many cases of the plague may have been transmitted by these kissing dances.)

A number of paintings were concerned with the danse macabre. For the most part, they were ugly and repulsive paintings. Death was represented by corpses with strips of rotting flesh. All painting and sculpture strove to be naturalistic, but with ugly exaggerations.

Along the Rhine Valley in Germany there were many reports of outbreaks of dancing madness. These were circle dances, with perhaps hundreds of people holding hands or in lines. They moved along with strange and distorted leaps and steps. The dance itself could go on for hours and might stretch out over many miles. Screaming, shouting, shaking, grimacing, the dance maniacs, as they were called, went on, drawing more and more spectators into the dance.

One trembling dance was called St. Vitus's dance. It was really a disease that doctors knew as *chorea major*, in which the muscles of the body contract and shake involuntarily. St. Vitus's dance spread throughout Germany. As though by a prearranged signal, whole villages would start the trembling and shaking St. Vitus's dance.

Children too performed this dance. One vivid story tells how one hundred children of the town of Erfurt in the year 1237 danced the ten miles all the way to Arnstadt. Many died of exhaustion along the way. The rest were unable to stop and continued to shake for the rest of their lives. Could this story and other similar ones have led to the legend of the *Pied Piper of Hamelin?* Perhaps the Pied Piper actually did represent the Grim Reaper.

In Italy dansomania took the form of the *tarantella*. Some say that the dance originated as the result of a bite of the tarantula. Others say that it started as a cure for the bite of a tarantula, since only this wild dance can cause the blood to circulate rapidly enough to avoid the fatal results of the spider's bite.

The most likely explanation seems to be that the tarantella is similar to many wild dances, from primitive times to modern day, that appear during particularly troubled times. Plagues, wars, famines, and other catastrophes call forth strong expressions of feelings in dance, as well as in the other arts. When people are excited and emotional, they look for outlets for their heightened feelings. The St. Vitus's dance and the tarantella are historically linked to the craze for dance marathons during World War I and the popularity

This etching by the Dutch artist Hondius shows several victims of St. Vitus's dance being held to control their wild movements.

of dancing in the Roaring '20s and the depression years of the '30s.

Recently medical science has offered a new explanation of dansomania. The wild dancing may have been, in part, uncontrolled muscular reactions in the arms and legs caused by eating ergot, a fungus that grows on rye grain. Since people in the Middle Ages mostly ate bread made from rye grain, there may well be a link between the disease and dansomania in the Middle Ages.

Dance in the Middle Ages

Although large numbers of people during the Middle Ages were caught up in the dance epidemics, many more were doing folk dances just for fun. Dancing was popular at fairs, village festivals, and seasonal celebrations.

Albrecht Dürer's print shows the lusty, vigorous style of peasant dancing of the Middle Ages.

These peasants are doing a circle dance around a tree outside the city walls.

The social dances that were most popular among all the people, rich and poor, through the eleventh century were chain and circle dances in which the performers moved, hand in hand, forming a circle or oval. These dances stemmed from the ancient magic dances of primitive times. For the most part, these dances, called choral dances, were stepping dances. The performers always sang as they danced. Instrumental accompaniments were almost never used.

From the many variations of the choral dance evolved the dance favorite of the time, the *carole*. The word itself means to dance in a circle to a vocal accompaniment. Basically the carole is a processional dance. As the dancers step forward, they turn first to one side, then to the other, beating one foot against the other as they do.

The carole, as a dance song, originated in the Provence area of France. It was usually performed in the month of

87

Of the many activities at peasants' fairs, the most popular was dancing.

May. Traveling minstrels introduced it all over Europe, where various peoples used it for different festivals and celebrations throughout the year. In Germany the carole was performed with many added hops and leaps. In England the word came to be used for song-dances that were performed in December to celebrate the shortest days of the year. This, of course, led to the Christmas carols, songs such as "Silent Night" and "O, Little Town of Bethlehem," that are now sung, though not danced, during the Christmas season.

Around the twelfth century, the dances of the peasants and of the nobles grew more and more different. The peasants, in general, stayed with the choral dance, which they danced gaily and spiritedly. Elements of pantomime were added to the processional part of the dance. There were imitations of animals in the dance and many references to courting movements as well as to sexual posturing. Dance tended toward the image, rather than the imageless, concept of dance. All the steps and gestures were performed vigorously and boldly.

The nobles, however, were evolving a totally different lifestyle. They looked down their noses at the lusty, gutsy dances of the peasants. Their new life-style involved codes of courtly life, romantic love, and chivalry. The steps of the simple carole became more precise, slow, and stately in the nobles' courts.

The most important influence on the dance of the nobles was the new concept of *cortezia*, or courtliness. It replaced

In contrast to the peasant dance, the nobles developed *cortezia*, or courtliness, in their dancing.

While most nobles danced in couples, they still occasionally did circle dances, as this woodcut shows.

the images of the peasant dance with imageless abstractions. Instead of pantomime, it emphasized stylized, symbolic movements.

While the peasants danced mostly in circles, the nobles tended to dance in couples. The couples often moved in procession, though without any pantomime. There was much more emphasis on grace and subtlety of movement than on release of emotion.

While the peasants danced in their simple work clothes that allowed full physical movement, the nobles wore full, elaborate costumes, heavy with velvets and brocades, and long pointed shoes on their feet. Men wore padding on their breasts. Instead of full coat sleeves, they had streamers hanging from their sleeves. Women wore exceedingly wide dresses, which hid the shape of their bodies. They wore their hair in high, complicated styles.

With the rise and growth of cities, a new class of merchants and tradesmen acquired wealth and position. They took up the dances of the nobles. They, too, danced the courtly, stately dances of the period.

A tradition of solo dancing was carried on during this time by the jugglers or joculators who worked for the nobles. They were professional performers, chosen for their grace, skill, and body build. Their dances were based on the old, expanded, extroverted types of primitive dance. Incorporated into these dances were elaborate hand and finger movements that they learned from the temple dancers who were captured in the Orient and brought to Europe.

The Tanzhaus

Among the many minstrels who performed in the nobles' courts were a group of Jews, who were also hired to entertain the aristocrats. These Jews came out of the crowded ghettos where, like all European Jews during the Middle Ages, they

A thirteenth-century Portuguese manuscript shows a minstrel, probably Jewish, dancing to the music of the psaltery.

were forced to live. Since living space was so limited, one room or building was set aside for festive celebrations, such as births, weddings, or joyous holidays. This place came to be called the *Tanzhaus*, or dance-house.

Dancing was an important part of many Jewish ceremonies and often lasted for several days. Since there were no set steps or patterns for many of the dances, there was confusion and many collisions in the limited space of the Tanzhaus. So there emerged dance leaders, similar to today's square-dance callers, who organized, taught, and led the dances in each Tanzhaus. They sang the dance melodies, taught the dance steps, and even developed new dances and steps. They became professional dance experts.

In time, some of these Jewish dance leaders left the ghettos. They traveled around as dance performers. Many were taken in as dance masters in the courts of the nobles. These Jewish dance masters are credited with working out many of the dance theories that became the basis of ballet and theatrical dancing.

7. The Birth of Ballet

A major revolution in human history, the Renaissance, occurred during the fifteenth and sixteenth centuries. It marked the end of the Middle Ages. The word means "rebirth." Renaissance, quite literally, was a rebirth of belief in the ancient Greek and Roman ideas and ideals and a newfound belief in the unique worth of each human being.

Many events and discoveries helped to bring about the great changes of the Renaissance. The Reformation, which began in 1517, led in time to the creation of the Protestant churches. Scientific advances in the basic understanding of the laws and nature of the universe changed people's concept of the world in which they lived. Technological inventions, such as the discovery of gunpowder and of printing with movable type, also affected people's lives. The voyages of exploration, by Columbus, Magellan, and others, widened trade and travel.

Many ambitious individuals rose to power, leadership, and great wealth through ownership of land or through trade or banking. Some became dukes; their sons, princes. They ruled the many city-states of Italy. And it was in the courts of these wealthy families, partly because of the new interest in art and partly to show off their riches, that dance changed from a social activity to theatrical entertainment.

Trionfi

Several leading families of the Renaissance tried to re-create the "triumphs," or *trionfi*, of ancient Rome. The Roman triumph was a magnificent parade. It was a high honor bestowed on a general upon his return from a victorious campaign. The marchers and chariots assembled in a field outside the city. The chariots were loaded with the weapons, captured soldiers and civilians, and other spoils of war. Legions of singing and dancing marchers surrounded each chariot. The opulently dressed general, seated on a throne, rode on the largest, most ornately decorated chariot, followed by the soldiers of his army.

Wealthy nobles in Renaissance Italy staged elaborate outdoor processions called *trionfi*.

An artist's conception of a float in one of the trionfi.

The Italian trionfi of the early Renaissance were splendid open-air processions, involving a number of separate wagons. Today we would call them floats. Each wagon was highly decorated around a central theme. The usual themes were either Roman gods or heroes, like Jupiter, Apollo, Caesar, and Augustus, or aspects of nature, such as the seasons, stars, planets, or animals. Costumed people riding on each wagon, or walking alongside, represented characters related to the theme. The performers danced, recited poems, and sang songs that were specially created for the trionfi.

The most talented people in the country participated in these pageants. Such artists as Leonardo da Vinci and Filippo Brunelleschi designed the sets. Outstanding poets, musicians, and dancers performed. Many of the leading nobles of the towns appeared on and around the wagons. The more lavish and grandiose the productions, the more immense and impressive the apparent wealth and power of the sponsor.

95

Balletti

While these spectacles were going on outdoors, similar indoor pageants were becoming fashionable. They started as entertainments put on by masked nobles or their servants between the courses of banquets. In fact, they were called *intromesso* ("something inserted") in Italy and *entremets* ("sweet course") in France.

The performers wore elaborate costumes and pantomimed various Greek and Roman legends. The ballrooms were decorated with complicated scenic effects to represent everything from fields covered with shrubs and trees to underwater grottoes, to the clouds of heaven. Groups of court dancers, moving in stately ways, formed geometrical patterns across the floor. The performances looked more like half-time football shows or military parading than dance performances.

Geometrical patterns were used in Renaissance dance because dance masters had to present spectacles that involved large numbers of nobles and servants who were untrained in dance. It would have been impossible to teach graceful movements or intricate dance steps to all of them. So the dance masters hit on the idea of merely arranging the performers into attractive, ever-changing squares, circles, and triangles on the vast floors of the nobles' ballrooms or banquet halls.

The geometry of the dance also reflected the Renaissance interest in mathematics and science. After the mystical, otherworld beliefs of the Middle Ages, the people of the Renaissance accepted the concept of a logical, rational universe, based on order, symmetry, and structure. The dance patterns symbolized this new world view.

The best-known intromesso was the wedding celebration for Gian Galeazzo, Duke of Milan, and Isabella of Aragon in

The Italian *balletti* grew more and more splendid and lavish as illustrated in this 1616 print of a performance in Florence. Note the ramp leading to the stage, and the arch, called a proscenium, around the stage.

1489. It is often referred to as the first ballet, or *balletti*, the name coming from the Italian *ballare*, which means "to dance."

This feast, which lasted some five hours, had the various courses brought in and served by dancers dressed as Greek gods. Jason and the Argonauts danced into the dining hall bringing the Golden Fleece, which was actually the roast-lamb course. The hunters Theseus and Atalanta brought in the wild boar to be carved. A dancing Iris brought peacocks. Triton brought fish. On it went until Bacchus served the wine. The meal ended with a wild dance in which everyone joined.

During the following years, the balletti became more and more lavish. As princes increased their wealth and power, they vied with each other to present the most extravagant entertainment. They offered bribes for the best dancing masters to plan the dancing. They bought the rarest and most expensive fabrics for the costumes. And they spared no cost to make the scenery and lighting as thrilling and spectacular as possible.

The dances of the Renaissance tended to be controlled and restrained, with grace and beauty as the ideals. The balletti strove for the dignity, serenity, balance, and repose that are so central to all Greek art. To the nobles of the fifteenth and sixteenth centuries, the world was well ordered, safe, and pleasant. Dance made the beauty and ordered structure of the world concrete and visible.

The long dreadful wars, the plagues, famines, and diseases that had claimed entire populations were over. The floods and hard times of the Middle Ages seemed to be gone. No longer was there a reason for dansomania. Dance no longer needed to provide an escape for these powerful emotions.

During the Renaissance, it became important in dance, as in the other arts, to have a set of rules. People strove to study and practice these rules in order to achieve perfection. Many of the wealthy families, then, turned to dancing masters to train them in dance, to invent new steps, and to choreograph the steps and patterns of the dance.

Dancing Masters

The teachings and books of the dancing masters created specific steps that were elegant and beautiful. They ruled out spontaneous and impulsive movements. Dance was to be restrained and refined. It was a skill to be studied and mastered.

One of the foremost dance masters was Guglielmo Ebreo, sometimes called William the Jew, who came out of the Tanzhaus tradition at the end of the Middle Ages.

Gugliemo Ebreo, shown here with two of his students, was a leading dancing master.

Little is known of his life except that he was born about 1440 in Pesaro on the east coast of Italy. His parents were Jews who had probably come from Spain. He grew up in the Pesaro ghetto where he very likely organized the dances and dancers in the Tanzhaus.

As a young man, Guglielmo left the ghetto and headed north to study with a leading dancer, Domenechino of Piacenza. After he finished his apprenticeship, he became famous as a dancer, musician, and teacher of the dance. Since he was the best and most popular dancing master of the day, he was hired to teach and present dance performances in the homes of the very wealthiest nobles.

Guglielmo set down the six basic skills of dance. They are *misuro*, the ability to keep time and dance in rhythm; *memoria*, the ability to recall the steps of a dance; *partire del terreno*, a knowledge of the space in which you dance; *aiere*, a

In sixteenth-century Venetian weddings it was customary for the dancing master to do the first dance with the bride, in place of the father.

This fifteenth-century drawing by an unknown Flemish artist shows the slow stately steps of the *basse danse*.

swaying and upward movement of the body; *maniera*, adapting the body to the movement of the feet; and *movemento corporeo*, graceful posture and carriage.

The most popular dance performed at the Renaissance courts was the *basse danse*, or bass dance. In fact, some call the fifteenth and early sixteenth centuries the age of the basse danse. It was quite literally a low dance, since the dancer's feet hardly left the floor as they went through the slow, stately steps of this dignified dance.

In contrast to this slow, gliding dance, the *saltarello*, "little leap," was an energetic, happy dance. It was sometimes called a high dance, because the feet were always being lifted off the floor with small leaps and jumps. It had a strong three-beat rhythm, and according to some, resembled the tarantella.

Finally there was the popular *piva*. The dancers used fast double steps in this dance to keep up with the rapid tempo of the music.

Le Ballet Comique de la Reine of 1581 is one of the first ballets to combine both dance and music.

The basse danse, saltarello, and piva were for their time quite revolutionary. They were part of a new dance style that aimed at precision and elegance, required the memorization of complex steps, and was judged by set standards for the quality of the dancing. These concepts became part of the foundation of ballet and all theatrical dancing.

Ballet Comique

Important to the development of ballet was the October 15, 1581, production of *Le Ballet Comique de la Reine*. Although it was performed in Paris, it was largely the work of Italians. The patron was Catherine de Médicis, Queen Mother of France, and a daughter of the wealthy, aristocratic Italian Medici family. She engaged the dance master Balthasar de Beaujoyeulx, an outstanding dancer and musician, born in Italy as Baldassarino da Belgiojoso.

Jacques Patain, a French artist, built the scenery and decorated the room. At one end, on a raised platform, sat the royal family. On another platform, at the opposite end of the hall, was the castle and gardens of the witch Circe. Along one side wall was a cave, and the gardens and woods of Pan were along the other. In one corner, surrounded by clouds and lit from the inside, sat the musicians. The musical score was composed by Sieur de Beaulieu especially for the occasion.

The ballet started with the overture at about ten in the evening. An actor entered the hall from Circe's castle and recited a long poem about the evil witch. He was followed by a procession of singing and dancing performers costumed like sirens and tritons.

Next came an elaborate float, like those seen in the trionfi, built to look like a fountain. Riding on the float were the twelve main dancers of the ballet, dressed like nymphs.

They stepped down to the floor and proceeded to pantomime the story of Circe and to form a succession of geometrical patterns.

On and on went the entertainment. A chariot was rolled in carrying the Four Virtues. A serpent dragged in another float with the goddess Pallas. Jupiter came in, riding on the head of an eagle. Circe and Jupiter mimed the climactic battle scene, ending with a powerful thunderbolt as Jupiter struck down the evil woman. All of the witch's victims danced for joy, and the ballet came to a close with a complicated figured dance of the nymphs.

Afterward, the dancers were presented to the King and Queen, and they went through a prepared routine of forty different patterns of squares, circles, and triangles in bewildering succession. At the conclusion, both the performers and spectators joined in social dancing.

Le Ballet Comique de la Reine was an overwhelming spectacle and a huge success. It cost three and a half million francs to put on, a considerable sum even to royalty. The large hall of the Petit-Bourbon Palace was filled with nine hundred spectators, and many more were turned away. The performance lasted five and a half hours, until three thirty in the morning.

Ballet has gone through many changes over the hundreds of years since the first balletti and the first *Ballet Comique.* Yet, the basic concept, the combination of dance and music in a dramatic presentation, of Renaissance court entertainments is very much a part of today's ballet and theatrical dance.

8. Steps to the Waltz

The Renaissance also influenced the growth and development of social dances. Many of the dances that arose as folk dances among the peasants and country people were gradually taken over by the nobles and aristocrats. Dances that began as rough, rude dances, related to magic themes or pantomimed forms, were tamed and polished by the wealthy bankers and landowners. The popular basse danse, saltarello, and piva underwent great changes during the Renaissance. Over the next centuries many other heavy-shoed peasant dances were changed into light, graceful dances as they moved from the peasants' taverns and village greens to the nobles' courts and ballrooms.

The Galliard

The most popular dance just before the Renaissance was the *galliard*. At first, it was a gay, lively country dance. As danced by the peasants, the galliard opened with a procession of men and women, like those of ancient, primitive dances. Then, as the women watched, the men danced before them, leaping and kicking. Next, the men watched as the women seductively danced away from them. Again, the men took the lead, advancing with even more vigor, followed by the women falling back even more demurely. This imitation of courtship patterns, distantly related to primitive fertility rites, went on, back and forth, until the musicians stopped playing.

The galliard was of interest to the wealthy gentry because it was gay and lively. But it was considered a little too rough for their taste. As it moved into the ballrooms and courts of Europe, the dance became smoother and tamer.

The Minuet

Besides the galliard, the other popular ballroom dances of the time were the *pavane*, the *sarabande*, and the *courante*. All of them showed, more or less, that they were derived from folk and primitive dances.

By the end of the seventeenth century, though, the dance masters and the trend-setters of the courts decided they needed a more perfect symbol of the elegance and refinement of the times. They found it in a dance, the *minuet*, as created at the royal court of Louis XIV in his spectacular palace at Versailles just outside Paris.

The minuet was an open couple dance, with a long list of strict rules for its proper execution. It required at all times a special bearing and posture that the noblemen and women had to learn. The dance was done with small, mincing steps, as the couple danced first to one side and then to the other. Forward and back they went, separating and then approaching each other. Holding hands, they gracefully glided past one another, going through a whole series of complex steps and patterns.

This illustration of the Minuet comes from Kellom Tomlinson's 1735 manual, *Art of Dancing*.

The minuet appealed greatly to the aristocrats of the time. They received instructions on dancing the minuet from the dancing masters and sent their children to learn it at dancing schools. Those who mastered the difficulties of the minuet danced with light, small, dainty steps. In fact, the name derives from the French words *pas menu*, meaning "small step." It was a dance that was well suited to the nobles in their patent-leather pumps and heavy costumes who were so eager to show how different they were from robust, earthy peasants.

The Waltz

By the middle of the eighteenth century people were beginning to tire of the minuet. The dance belonged to a society that was strictly structured and carefully regulated. Now, in the 1750s, new ideas of democracy and liberty were sweeping across Europe. These new currents were doing away with the courts of Europe, even as they were eliminating the courtly minuet.

The courts of Europe had long been seats of power. Dance and the other arts—painting, sculpture, music, and literature—reflected the strength of the aristocrats. But by 1750 the nobles had begun to lose much of their power. Their art had become hollow, uninspired imitations of past glories.

The new power was in the hands of the emerging bourgeoisie, the so-called middle class. Merchants, bankers, shipowners, and manufacturers were now the leaders of society. They had new ideas of simplicity and naturalism. The arts turned away from the studied elegance of the past. Artists sought to capture the earthy, expressive, and emotional content of the natural world. Fashions became more youthful and exuberant. The natural beauty of peasant and folk art was greatly admired.

At first, the bourgeoisie took over the dances of the courtly world. But these dances seemed artificial and mannered. They wanted new dances to put an end to the carefully learned and measured steps and to replace them with more joyful, intense movement. They began to dance so-called peasant dances at fancy balls.

One such dance was the *ländler*. The ländler was one part of an old peasant courtship dance of the Alps of Austria and southern Germany. It was named after the Ländl district of the Austrian mountains. The full dance was known as the

Schuhplattler, and it can still be seen in some of the high mountain villages of that region.

The ländler was a slow couple dance. It was always done in three-beat time with a heavy accent on the first beat, the typical oom-pah-pah, oom-pah-pah rhythmic pattern of the waltz. It was usually danced to a series of separate melodies, each one calling forth a different dance figure.

The rhythms of the ländler were brought from the Austrian Alps to Vienna by the musicians on the barges that

In the ländler, an Austrian peasant dance, the boys and girls twist around each other's raised arms. *Austrian National Tourist Office*

sailed down the Danube River. And it was in the suburban inns and beer gardens of that city that the rustic peasant dance underwent the transformations that made it into the *waltz*, the most popular dance of all time.

In the dance halls of Vienna, the waltz became lighter, with more emphasis on charm and grace. The tempo became slightly faster, more suited to the city dancers' smooth-soled shoes and pumps than to the peasants' heavy hobnailed boots, more suited, too, to the polished floors of the dance halls than to the stone floors of the taverns.

In its basic form the waltz keeps the three-beat rhythm of the ländler. The couples follow a circular path around the ballroom as they turn in each other's arms. The movement is often compared to the solar system, with each planet spinning around itself as it moves through its orbit around the sun.

An 1816 dance manual shows the various steps of the waltz.

This lithograph from 1844 shows a couple doing the waltz.

The waltz was a comfortable, easy dance to do, with just one basic step. Simple and natural in style, it did not depend on the tutelage of the dancing masters.

Introduced in Vienna around 1769, the waltz quickly swept through Austria and the rest of Europe. In a few years the minuet disappeared entirely. The literature of dance bears testimony to the death of the minuet and the birth of the waltz. The last of the many dance manuals on the minuet, M. J. de Chavanne's *Principes du Menuet*, was published in 1767. The first of the flood of books on the waltz, C. von Zangeis' *Etwas uber das Waltzen*, was published in 1772.

A dance floor filled with waltzing couples creates a beautiful vision.

During the remaining years of the eighteenth century, the waltz continued to grow in appeal and popularity. Everyone, everywhere was dancing the waltz. A survey done in France in 1797 showed that there were 684 public dance halls in Paris alone, and in each one, the waltz was the favorite dance by far!

By the early years of the nineteenth century, a number of outstanding Austrian composers began writing waltz melodies for the small orchestras found in every restaurant and dance hall in Europe. The first of these composers was Josef Lanner (1801–1843). He did much to establish the musical form of the waltz. But his influence was slight compared with that of the various members of Vienna's Strauss family. Johann I (1804–1849) started the tradition. He was bested by his son, Johann II (1825–1899), who came to be known as the Waltz King. During the 1860s Johann II wrote a succession of the world's best-known waltzes, including "The Blue Danube," "Tales from the Vienna Woods," "Wine, Women and Song." His brothers, Josef (1827–1870) and Eduard (1835–1916), were also famous, both as waltz composers and as leaders of orchestras that performed for dances. The waltz tradition of the Strauss family ended with Johann III (1886–1939), the son of Eduard.

In the waltz, the women fling their long, full skirts about as they turn around the room. In fact, the billowing and swirling skirts of the women make the waltz one of the beautiful visions of this period. Sometimes the woman held up one corner of her skirt so that it would not be stepped on. Many an extra squeeze or kiss was stolen behind the raised skirt.

In Germany, the waltz spawned the *schottische*, which was related to the original waltz but was gayer and more active. In America, the popular version of the waltz was the *Boston*, which was danced at a slower tempo than the Viennese waltz.

The waltz reigned supreme wherever people came to-

Modern dancers add their own extra steps to the waltz. *P/I's Dance Charisma*

gether to dance. Only one dance, the *polka*, offered it any rivalry. The polka started out as a peasant dance in Bohemia (now Czechoslovakia) in the 1830s and soon spread throughout Europe and America. It is a lively, turning couple dance, done in two-beat time, with vigorous movements of the feet, head, trunk, and arms. In dance halls and at the balls, it served largely as a contrast to the more sedate waltz, which continued to dominate social dancing.

For some 150 years, from the second half of the eighteenth century through the entire nineteenth century, the waltz remained the most popular dance. It symbolized an entire age of stability and permanence, of fixed and unchanging social and economic structures and institutions. Only with the coming of the twentieth century, the eruption of World War I, and the Communist Revolution in Russia did the waltz lose its preeminent position.

The only dance that approached the waltz in popularity was the polka, a lively dance done with vigorous movements.

9. Classical Ballet

By the year 1640, theaters were being built with a raised platform stage, usually with a ramp leading up from the audience. Because an arch, called a proscenium, now framed the stage, many advances in theater craft were possible. The audience could not see backstage. Special lighting and mechanisms for achieving spectacular stage effects were introduced. Of particular importance to dance was the ability to "fly" the dancers up into the air by systems of hidden wires.

Ballet moved out óf the ballrooms and into these new theaters. The stage focused attention on the individual dancers. Over the years a number of outstanding professional performers made significant contributions to the development of ballet.

Of the many leading dancers and choreographers who introduced reforms in the years before the nineteenth-century flowering of classic ballet, three figures are of particular importance.

Marie Sallé (1707–1756) fought against the ballet conventions of the time. She wore only a simple muslin gown modeled on the ancient Greek tunic instead of fancy costumes. She let her hair fall naturally and wore no jewels or ornaments. She added a personal, emotional element to her dancing that had not been part of traditional ballet.

Marie Camargo (1710–1770) rivaled Sallé as the leading dancer of the eighteenth century. Camargo shortened the skirt, removed the heel from dancing shoes, and established the 90-degree turnout of the legs as a requirement of ballet dancing. She was famous in her time also for the effortless speed of her dancing and her *entrechat quatre,* in which she leaped and crossed her legs four times while in the air.

The choreographer Jean Georges Noverre (1727–1810) strove to make his dances as artistic as possible. He called only for gestures and movements that fit the character and put an end to the use of masks. He chose costumes that were appropriate to the time and place of the ballet's story. Many dance scholars feel that nineteenth-century ballet grew from Noverre's innovations.

The movements of an eighteenth-century ballet dancer were very limited by her costume.

Choreographer Arthur Saint-Léon's most famous ballet is *Coppélia*. Here a young girl has convinced Dr. Coppelius that a life-sized doll he made has come to life. *Photo: Susan Cook; Eglevsky Ballet Co.*

Above: Raymonda, with choreography by Marius Petipa and music by Alexander Glazunov, is one of the best-known nineteenth-century ballets. *Photo: Sandy Underwood; Cincinnati Ballet Co.*

Left: With their light, short skirts and blocked ballet slippers, women became the dominant stage dancers in nineteenth-century ballet. *Photo: Sandy Underwood; Cincinnati Ballet Co.*

Nineteenth-Century Ballet

Some of the greatest and most famous of all ballets were created in the middle years of the nineteenth century. Although artistically this was the height of the romantic century, these ballet masterpieces are called classic ballets, because of their lasting quality.

The choreographers were extremely original and imaginative in planning and designing the ballets. Their stories usually had supernatural, rustic, and peasant themes, or were exotic tales of the Orient or Africa. Among the leading choreographers of the time were Carlo Blasis (1795–1878), Arthur Saint-Léon (1821–1870), and Marius Petipa (1822–1910).

A number of brilliant ballet stars, famous for the skill and beauty of their dancing, emerged during this period. The best known of these dancers were Maria Taglioni (1804–1884), Fanny Elssler (1810–1884), Carlotta Grisi (1819–1899), and the one man in the group, Jules Perrot (1810–1892).

In these ballets, women, for the first time, assumed a more important role than men dancers. In the past, the women's heavy clothes and heeled shoes confined them to very limited movements, while the men's simpler outfits allowed them to be much more active. With the introduction of lighter, shorter skirts for the dancers, of blocked ballet slippers, and of toe dancing, the women became the dominant stage dancers. The men were largely relegated to lifting and supporting the women, with only a rare solo turn.

These changes in ballet reflected some of the new ideas spreading through Europe at the beginning of the nineteenth century. The revolutions in America and France at the end of the eighteenth century attempted to create political systems that guaranteed justice and equality for every citizen. Philosophers and thinkers wrote impassioned tracts on democracy and freedom. Writers and artists glorified the common people. Anything that related to the life of the peasants, such as country life or nature, was admired and imitated.

The high idealism with which the century began, though, soon turned to disappointment. The promises and hopes for a new era of justice and prosperity were not being realized. Napoleon, a hero of the French Revolution, destroyed many of the newly won gains when he declared himself Emperor of France. The industrial revolution, instead of improving living conditions and meeting people's needs, created new inequalities. The factories and mills restricted the people who worked in them and polluted both the cities and the countryside.

In nineteenth-century ballet, men were largely confined to lifting and supporting the women, as shown in this scene from *The Sleeping Beauty*. *Photo: Susan Cook; Eglevsky Ballet Co.*

People reacted to these unpleasant realities by turning away from the real world. The artists found new subject matter in fantasy and make-believe, in spirits, ghosts, and fairies. Another direction of escape was to the distant past. Archeological explorations during this period had unearthed many objects and art works from ancient civilizations. Nineteenth-century artists also drew inspiration from these sources.

During the nineteenth century, many Europeans met people from Asia, Africa, and other faraway places for the first time. They were attracted by these men and women whose appearance and way of life were so different from their own. The arts, including dance, often chose remote settings and exotic characters to satisfy this interest and curiosity.

Above all, the nineteenth century was a time of emotion and passion. Feelings and instincts were much more trusted than rational, intellectual thought. Love was the most powerful of all drives, and woman the object of all affection.

Each of these new ways of thinking and perceiving the world had a direct influence on the ballets of the time, especially in the themes of the dances and the roles played by men and women.

The first two full-length ballets that stand out as nineteenth-century masterpieces are *La Sylphide* and *Giselle.*

La Sylphide was first performed on March 12, 1882, at the Paris Opéra, which was then known as the Théâtre de l'Académie Royale de Musique. The ballet was conceived and choreographed by Filippo (later Philippe) Taglioni (1777–1871) to suit the very considerable talents of his daughter, Maria Taglioni.

Maria Taglioni was the first of the world-famous ballerinas. She became the center of a worshipful cult. Enthusiasts pointed to the perfection of her body, the great distances she covered in her leaps, the smoothness of her glides, and the lightness and grace of her movements. It was said that she danced as though the law of gravity had been suspended, and that when she was in the air for a leap she was reluctant to return to earth. Painters and sculptors tried to capture the beauty of her dancing body in their art. Poets and novelists tried to describe in words the electrifying effect of her stage presence.

Taglioni danced the part of La Sylphide, a nymph or otherworldly spirit, taken from northern mythology. The story is typical of the ballets of that time. It is largely told through pantomime and concerns the love of a spirit for James, a handsome Scottish lad. The ballet traces the difficulties the lovers face and ends with the death of the spirit, in James' arms, and her ascent to heaven.

Although *La Sylphide* was popular for many years, it has largely disappeared from today's repertoire. A different and much later ballet, *Les Sylphides*, is often performed today.

Giselle, though, has remained one of the most popular of all ballets. It has been kept alive and passed down from generation to generation by several dance companies, notably those of Paris, Leningrad, and Moscow.

Giselle was first presented on June 28, 1841, also at the Paris Opéra. Jean Coralli (1779–1854), the official choreographer for the Paris Opéra, did most of the choreography, but Jules Perrot, a dancer himself and husband of the leading ballerina, Carlotta Grisi, choreographed the role of Giselle.

The heroine, Giselle, is a carefree village girl who falls in love with a woodchopper. When she discovers that the woodchopper is really the Duke of Albrecht, she gives way to despair and goes mad, because she knows that they cannot marry. At the end of a powerfully emotional dance, she seizes Albrecht's sword and plunges it into her heart. The first act ends as she falls lifeless into her mother's arms. The grief-stricken villagers look on in shock. Traditionally, the perform-

Madame Taglioni.

Maria Taglioni was the first of the world-famous nineteenth-century ballerinas.

A typical theme of nineteenth-century ballet is the love between a spirit woman and a mortal man. In *Swan Lake* the woman has been turned into a swan by the evil magician. *Photo: Sandy Underwood; Cincinnati Ballet Co.*

Marius Petipa, shown dancing with ballerina Barie-Guy Stephan in this old print, choreographed the famous ballets *Swan Lake, The Sleeping Beauty,* and *The Nutcracker.*

ers do not acknowledge the applause here but remain frozen in place as the curtains open and close.

After her death, Giselle becomes one of the Wilis, the ghosts of girls who died before marriage. The cruel Queen of the Wilis bids Giselle to dance Albrecht to his death. Giselle tries to protect him, but the other Wilis continue the dance until Albrecht is weak and dying. Just before he dies, though, the dawn breaks, and the Wilis must return to their graves. As Giselle, too, slips into her grave, Albrecht rushes toward it and falls on the ground as the ballet ends.

Such romantic ballets are wonderful to watch. The dancers are beautifully made up and costumed, and the stage sets and the lighting very effectively create the illusion of the various scenes. The stage effects, such as La Sylphide rising to heaven or Giselle disappearing into the grave, are cleverly done.

The themes are often the same: a spirit woman in love with a mortal man. And the women, dancing on toes, appear

125

Swan Lake, with choreography by Marius Petipa, is one of the all-time favorites of ballet fans. *Photo: Sandy Underwood; Cincinnati Ballet Co.*

light and delicate and free-floating, perfectly fitting the romantic view of women as ethereal beings.

But this glorious period of ballet did not last long. Around 1860 it began to decline. The reasons for the decline can be found in the ballets themselves. Many of the new dances were rigid. They were created to formula. Consequently, they were devoid of real expression or deep feeling.

The dancing was filled with high leaps and amazing *entrechats*. But the dancers mainly used these steps to display their technique, not to express the character or meaning of the ballet. The costumes, too, were not related to the setting or time of the dance. The women wore tutus. Their hair was prepared in the latest fashion. And they were heavily bedecked with jewels, whether or not they fit the role.

The stories of the ballets were told through pantomime. In order to provide dance opportunities, each ballet was arranged to include a section of divertissements, or specialty dances. Such artifices as a ball, a village celebration, a noble's court, or some similar situation allowed the choreographer to introduce a variety of character dances.

The music for the ballets was usually provided by staff composers who worked for the various ballet companies. Most often the choreographer would plan the entire ballet and then give the composer a rundown of the musical

Many generations of boys and girls have "oohed" and "ahed" at the appearance of the Christmas tree in *The Nutcracker* ballet since its first performance in 1892. *Photo: Sandy Underwood; Cincinnati Ballet Co.*

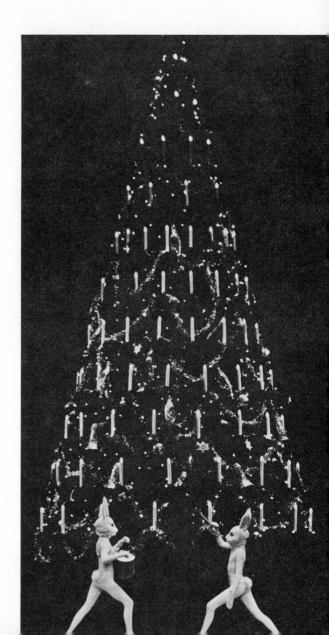

requirements: 32 measures of slow four-beat music, followed by a three-minute waltz, 12 bells to indicate the chiming of a clock, 128 measures in fast two-beat time, and so on. The music, which was written to be performed by a symphony orchestra, was usually of the same low quality as the choreography.

Among the few ballets from the second half of the nineteenth century that still survive are *Coppélia* (1870), with music by Léo Delibes and choreography by Arthur Saint-Léon, and the three well-known ballets to scores by Peter Ilyich Tchaikovsky, *Swan Lake* (1876), *The Sleeping Beauty* (1890), and *The Nutcracker* (1892), all choreographed by Marius Petipa. They survive because the composers and choreographers rose above the restrictions that fettered ballet at the time.

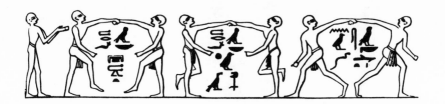

10. Ballet in the Twentieth Century

"I don't want my Mimotchka to be a hoofer!" declared Michel Fokine's father when it was first suggested that the boy be given ballet lessons. (Mimotchka is a nickname for Michel.) But Michel did become a dancer and choreographer and went on to set a new course for twentieth-century ballet.

Michel Fokine (1880–1942) liked the idea of ballet school right from the start. He had always enjoyed dancing and watching dancers. Despite his father's rather weak objections, he entered the Russian government's Imperial Ballet School at the age of nine.

One year later Michel appeared in his first ballet production. His father bought expensive box seats to show his approval, and because he wanted to see Michel perform once before he completely lost his failing sight. Unfortunately, Michel's role called for him to stand behind an immense pitcher and move it from place to place for changes of scene. He was almost completely hidden during most of the ballet, but this did little to lessen his father's pride.

The Imperial Ballet School was strict and demanding. "Back straight! Turn out! Head up! Arms curved! Fingers together! Eyes front! Stretch! Pull! Leap! Again, again,

The training of ballet dancers, in the past as well as today, is strict and demanding. *Chautauqua Dance Department*

The aim of dance training is to produce a beautiful, controlled instrument for the dance. *Joyce Trisler Danscompany*

again!" It seems, sometimes, as though the person giving the ballet class, usually an older or retired dancer, is driving the students without mercy. Yet, no one has found a better way to turn a youngster's body into a beautiful, controlled instrument for the dance.

Even as a student, Fokine wondered why it was necessary to teach all the unchanging positions and movements of ballet, and why they had to be taught in exactly the same way. He did everything that his teachers required, but he had many questions in his own mind. He never raised these

Choreographers who followed Michel Fokine accepted his point that ballet gestures should be natural and expressive, as seen in this modern version of *Cinderella* choreographed by André Eglevsky and Jane Miller. *Photo: Susan Cook; Eglevsky Ballet Co.*

questions because he knew what the answer would be: "This is what we were taught. Such is the tradition. Hold your back! Point your toes! And keep still!"

Fokine graduated at the age of eighteen. He immediately became a member of the Imperial Ballet Company and started to teach at the school. His critical thinking, though, did not stop. At the age of twenty-four, Fokine wrote a letter to the directors of the Ballet Company. He suggested five ways in which ballet could and should be improved. Fokine's five points have become the cornerstones of modern ballet.

First, movements for each dance should be created especially for that dance. They should strive to express the meaning and create the mood for that work. It was not enough to string together separate movements from the dance class to make a ballet.

Second, the story of the ballet should unfold naturally. There should be a perfect blend between dance and music. To use mime for the storytelling part of the ballet and dance during the divertissements destroyed the unity of the work.

Fokine's third point related to the gestures used to carry the story line of ballet. Expressive mime gestures should grow from the stage situation and the characters involved. He believed in avoiding such old clichés of mime as hands crossed over the chest to represent mother and shaking a fist at heaven for anger.

Fourth, Fokine wanted the corps de ballet, the dancers of the chorus or ensemble who have no solo dances, to be made an integral part of the dance. They should not serve as a movable backdrop for the soloist. Rather, they should help to unfold the story.

And finally, Fokine held that ballet should be a union in which choreography, music, story, scenery, costume, and stage effects should all be integrated to heighten the emotional content and clarify the meaning of the dance.

133

Fokine's suggestions for the reform of ballet were part of the revolutionary spirit in Russia at the time, which reached its climax in the unsuccessful revolution of 1905. During that eventful year, the workers of the country forced the Czar, Nicholas II, to introduce new freedoms and reforms and to establish an elected congress, called the Duma.

Fokine and the other dancers, as well as actors, painters, and musicians, were caught up in the struggle for justice and equality. They began to speak of the need for freedom in the arts. For the first time, dancers and ballet students took courses at St. Petersburg University and read serious books on politics and philosophy. In October 1905, the dancers of the Imperial Ballet drafted a set of demands that included higher salaries, more free time, the right to choose the company manager, and the return of Petipa as choreographer. (He had been choreographer for the company since 1870 but had been

Fokine believed that choreography, music, story, scenery, costumes, and stage effects should be integrated. *Photo: Herb Migdoll; Christian Holder, Charthel Arthur, and Gary Chryst of The Joffrey Ballet.*

removed earlier in 1905.) They spoke of going on strike if their demands were not met.

The directors of the ballet took stern measures against the dancers. The refused to consider their requests, they forbade them from meeting, and they applied so much pressure that the dancers finally gave up their demands. They lost their struggle, just as the political gains won by the workers of Russia were soon withdrawn. Conditions returned to those that existed before the Revolution.

In spite of the objections of his superiors, Fokine, who was doing some choreography for the students at the school and for the Imperial Ballet, gradually began to introduce some of his new ideas. When he did a ballet set in ancient Greece, he studied books and pictures to learn how the early Greeks dressed and how they moved. He incorporated this information into the dance, even though it required costumes and steps that were not a part of traditional ballet. He introduced tumbling and acrobatics, which had never been used in classical ballet. He choreographed one dance in which the performers leaped onto the stage carrying torches with real flames that shot high in the air and threw off sparks in all directions.

In 1909 Fokine joined Sergei Diaghilev's Ballets Russes. Diaghilev (1872–1929) had a varied career in the arts—as an organizer of art exhibits, editor of an art magazine, and an official of the Imperial Theatres. In 1909 he presented the first of several seasons of Russian ballet in Paris, with choreography by Fokine, music by Russia's leading composers (such as Igor Stravinsky), and décor by Russia's leading artists (such as Alexandre Benois).

Fokine's dances fall into four categories: Ancient Greek, Oriental, a style based on the waltz and other ballroom dances of the early nineteenth century, and Russian. He used each style to evoke a particular place or time.

In the works he choreographed, he asked the dancers to use a flexible and supple back instead of the stiff spine of traditional ballet. The arm and leg movements that he suggested were swifter and freer than those used in the past. He replaced formal symmetry with free symmetry in both individual dances as well as in overall staging. He put dancers on platforms so they could be on different planes. Male dancers had steps and movements that went far beyond the usual lifting and supporting of the women. And he created shorter, one-act ballets to replace the evening-long ballets of the past.

Fokine's first famous ballet, composed in 1909, was *Les Sylphides*, which he originally called *Chopiniana*. He choreographed it to six piano pieces by Chopin that had been arranged for orchestra. Although it took only three days to do the choreography, Fokine boasted later in his life that he never forgot one of the steps or movements of the ballet. *Les Sylphides* is different from most of his storytelling ballets. It is an abstract ballet, with no plot or narrative line.

Over the following years, Fokine created a series of brilliant ballets for Diaghilev's Ballets Russes. Some of the more important ones were *Schéhérazade* (1910), *The Firebird* (1910), *Spectre de la Rose* (1911), *Petrouchka* (1911), and *Daphnis and Chloë* (1912).

Perhaps Fokine's most popular ballet is *Petrouchka*. It is set at a colorful, crowded Russian country fair. A Magician plays the flute to bring his three puppets, the Moor, the Ballerina, and Petrouchka, to life. It is soon apparent that Petrouchka is in love with the Ballerina, who spurns him for the handsome Moor. Petrouchka and the Moor fight over the Ballerina's love, and Petrouchka is killed. The crowd expresses its shock but is calmed by the Magician who assures everyone that Petrouchka and the others are only puppets.

Right: Fokine's most popular ballet is *Petrouchka,* created for Diaghilev's Ballets Russes in 1911. *Photo by Herb Migdoll; Christian Holder and Charthel Arthur of The Joffrey Ballet*

Below: Notice Petrouchka's turned-in toes—a highly unusual position in traditional ballet. *Photo: Herb Migdoll; Charthel Arthur, Christian Holder, and Gary Chryst of The Joffrey Ballet*

Petrouchka is a short, one-act ballet. All the people responsible for its creation, Fokine, the choreographer, Stravinsky, the composer, and Alexandre Benois, the set and costume designer, worked together. The corps de ballet is costumed as visitors to the fair, such as nursemaids, coachmen, and gypsies. Each group has its own set of characteristic dances.

The most dramatic break with tradition in *Petrouchka* is the difference between the choreography for the Moor and for Petrouchka. The Moor, who is a strong character, dances in the traditional way, *en dehors*, or turned out. It contributes to the strength and force of his character. But Petrouchka dances *en dedans*, or tuned in. The unusual position makes very clear Petrouchka's weak, frightened personality.

After Fokine left the Ballets Russes, his ideas were carried forward by Vaslav Nijinsky (1890–1950). Nijinsky was doubtless one of the greatest dancers of our time and Diaghilev's biggest star. Nijinsky choreographed only four ballets. The best known are *The Afternoon of a Faun* (1912) to the music of Claude Debussy and *The Rite of Spring (Le Sacre du Printemps)* to the music of Igor Stravinsky.

Nijinsky got many of his dance ideas from ballets that were choreographed by Fokine. He did not contribute much that was new and original. He had a poor understanding of music. And he had great difficulty in expressing himself and communicating with the dancers. Yet, he introduced a new freedom into dance that did much to advance the art.

The world premiere of Nijinsky's *The Rite of Spring* took place in Paris on May 29, 1913. It was one of the most scandalous evenings in the history of dance. As the curtains parted, a few members of the audience began to titter. Instead of lightly clad dancers, they saw heavily costumed performers dressed in peasant garb and clumsy boots. The laughter changed to hisses and boos as the dancers, instead of the more customary movements, did awkward jumps in place with toes touching and knees knocking together. Some members of the audience became very noisy as they attempted to drown out the pounding, throbbing, and at times violent Stravinsky musical score.

The uproar was so loud that the dancers were unable to hear the complex rhythm of the music. Nijinsky climbed on a chair in the wings and shouted out the beats to the struggling dancers.

Although the audience grew even more restive, and there were some loud arguments and violent fights in the theater, the ballet was performed in its entirety. Legend has it, however, that some members of the audience stormed backstage at the end. Nijinsky, Stravinsky, and Pierre Monteux, who conducted the orchestra, hid from the mob in a backstage men's room. Later they made their escape through an open window.

Despite these violent beginnings, twentieth-century ballet has gone on to become one of the most popular of the arts. Within the last decades, dozens of new ballet companies have sprung up all over the United States. Among all the companies performing now, a few stand out for their contributions to the development of ballet.

The New York City Ballet is one of the world's leading companies. To a great extent, it expresses the artistic vision of its choreographer and guiding artistic force, George Balanchine.

Balanchine was born Gheorghi Melitonovitch Balantchivadze in St. Petersburg (now Leningrad), Russia, in 1904. Since his mother came from a military family, it was assumed that he would chose the army as a career. One of the directors of the Imperial Ballet School, though, suggested that he try out for entrance to the school. Against his will,

Gheorghi auditioned. He was accepted and began his studies in 1914.

At first he was a poor student. He found it very hard to get used to the strict discipline of ballet training and even ran away from school once. But in the second year, when he began to have opportunities to perform, he became much more interested in ballet. Conditions at the school, though, were very bad. Because of World War I and the 1917 Russian Revolution, there was no heat in the classrooms and little food for the young dancers to eat.

On graduation, in 1921, Gheorghi tried his hand at some choreography but was reprimanded for putting on such shocking, erotic dances. Between the disapproval of the officials and the chaotic, repressive conditions in Russia at the time, Gheorghi was only too glad to leave with a small ballet company to perform in Germany.

The first morning out on the steamship to Germany, the dancers entered the dining room before any of the other passengers. Each table was already set with a basket of bread and rolls. The hungry dancers ate all the bread and rolls from three different tables before they sat down at a fourth table for breakfast.

From Germany the dancers went to Paris, where Diaghilev's Ballets Russes was performing. Gheorghi and some of the other dancers auditioned for Diaghilev and were taken into the company. The first thing Diaghilev did was simplify Gheorghi's name to its present George Balanchine. One month later, when Nijinsky left the company, Balanchine was made choreographer for the Ballets Russes. In his four years with Diaghilev, Balanchine turned out a number of dances that are still popular today: *The Nightingale* (1926), *Apollon Musagete* (1928), and *The Prodigal Son* (1929).

After Diaghilev's death, Balanchine did choreography for various opera houses in Europe. In 1933 he was invited to come to the United States to organize a ballet school and company. On New Year's Day, 1934, the School of American Ballet opened with twenty-five students. The first student performance was given on June 9, 1934; the first professional performances were given in December of that year. These performances were highly successful. They were the first of many more performances under the artistic direction of Balanchine. In 1948 the performing part of the school, which had undergone several changes of name, became the New York City Ballet and quickly moved to the forefront of ballet companies throughout the world.

According to Balanchine, "the material of dance is dance itself." His works do not usually tell stories or overwhelm the viewer with stage effects and dramatic spectacles. They are usually plotless and classical, depending for their effect on the sheer beauty of the dancers moving in space. Among the more popular of his later ballets are *Agon* (1957), *Stars and Stripes* (1958), *Union Jack* (1976), *Vienna Waltzes* (1977), and *Kammermusik II* (1978).

Balanchine and the New York City Ballet have had a major impact on ballet in America and throughout the world. But the company is but one among many important ballet companies that attract large audiences and produce excellent programs of both old and new works.

The American Ballet Theatre tours widely, both in the United States and abroad. The company makes frequent use of guest stars as performers and of guest choreographers. Performances include classic ballets, as well as many outstanding modern ballets. The brilliance of their production has won many fans to ballet.

Robert Joffrey (born 1930) directs the Robert Joffrey Ballet, a slightly smaller company than either the New York City Ballet or the American Ballet Theatre. Joffrey's exuberant young dancers perform a wide range of dances. They are

141

equally at home in classic ballet, in jazz dances, and in dances with the flavor of Spanish flamenco.

Alvin Ailey (born 1931) formed his own dance company in 1957. His unique contributions are to seek out a common ground between ballet and modern dance and to express the black experience in theatrical dance.

Total theater is the aim of Alwin Nikolais (born 1912), choreographer, composer, and director of the Nikolais Dance Theatre. By carefully planning the lighting, the costumes, the scenery, and the sound (often of his own composition), as well as the dancers' movements, Nikolais creates a variety of magical effects. It is particularly striking to see his dancers completely enveloped in costumes that stretch and shift as they move.

In addition to these companies with national and international reputations, almost every large city in the United States has its own ballet company. It is a sign of the vigor of ballet in America that many of these are new groups formed

Twyla Tharp is one of the guest choreographers who makes dances for the American Ballet Theatre. *Twyla Tharp Dance Foundation*

Above: Alvin Ailey seeks, in his choreography, to find a common ground between ballet and modern dance. *Photo: Donald Moss; Alvin Ailey Dance Theater*

Right: The Alvin Ailey Dance Theater expresses the black experience in its dances. *Photo: Jack Mitchell; Alvin Ailey Dance Theater*

143

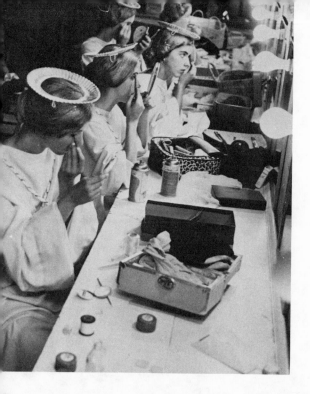

Left: "Five minutes, please," the stage manager calls out, as the dancers in a regional ballet company finish applying makeup. *Chautauqua Dance Company*
Below: Advanced girls dance on *pointes,* but boys seldom use this technique. *Photo: Chautauqua Dance Department*

within the last ten or twelve years. The dancers, choreographers, and productions of the best regional ballet companies rank with some of the top companies in the world.

Ballet today is, in many ways, very different from the ballet of the past. Yet the study of ballet has remained essentially the same since the first formal ballet instruction was given by French dancing masters nearly three hundred years ago. In fact, almost all the exercises, steps, and movements are still called by their French names, such as *plié* (knee bend), *relevé* (rising up tall on the ball of the foot or toes), *arabesque* (a pose with one foot raised), and even *révérence* (a bow to the teacher at the end of class and to the audience at the end of a performance).

Most ballet teachers are either dancers themselves or retired dancers. They usually agree that eight is an ideal age to start formal ballet training, even though many excellent dancers started their studies well after their eighth birthday.

Most beginning ballet students take one hour of class instruction per week. The class is ideally held in a large, airy room with a smooth wooden floor, a piano, a mirror covering one or more walls, and a *barre*, a wooden bar about waist high, along a wall.

The methods of ballet instruction vary considerably from teacher to teacher and change also with the age and level of advancement of the students. Basically, though, each class is divided into three parts.

First, there is work at the *barre*. The young dancers lightly hold on to the *barre* for balance as they go through a series of exercises under the direction of the teacher. The exercises serve as a warm-up, help develop correct posture and position, stretch and strengthen the muscles, and teach some of the basic positions and movements of ballet.

After the *barre*, the students move to *centre*, the open, central area of the dance studio. Here the teacher leads them

145

in exercises to develop balance without the support of the *barre* and to do more elaborate and extended movements than were done at the *barre*.

For the final section, the teacher creates different series or combinations of movements for the students to do. This is sometimes called *temps lié*. The students are asked to make a sequence of the various positions and movements they practiced earlier in the class.

Traditionally, when the dance class ends, the girls curtsy and the boys bow to the teacher in the *révérence*.

At the beginning, boys and girls are taught together. But as they advance, there are differences in instruction. After two or more years, at about age eleven, girls begin to dance on *pointes*, on their toes. They wear special shoes with wooden blocks in the tips to support them.

Boys are not taught to dance on *pointes*, since male dancers almost never use this technique. Instead, the boys work to develop the special features of male dancing—high leaps, turns in the air, and beating their legs together during a leap.

As students advance, they also increase the number of classes they take each week. By the time they are in their teens, serious students may be taking ten or more classes every week. And any youngsters who go on to become professional dancers continue taking classes throughout their careers to warm up each day and to keep their muscles and bodies in top condition.

Almost every city and town has a ballet school. Since there is no license required or government supervision, anyone can open a school. Some schools are run by people who are not properly trained in ballet. Studying in one of these schools can do more harm than good to a young dancer. In general, the schools taught by professional ballet dancers,

The young ballet student today is part of a dance tradition that goes back hundreds of years. *Photo: Chautauqua Dance Department*

either active or retired, or run by professional ballet companies provide the finest instruction.

Some of the best serious teaching is offered at schools connected with ballet companies. The more talented students are given opportunities to appear in their productions. And the most advanced and gifted students have an excellent chance of eventually becoming members of the professional company.

Many students of ballet, though, have little thought of becoming professional dancers. They study dance to develop their bodies, to be better able to express their feelings and emotions through dance, and to heighten their appreciation and enjoyment of the art. No matter what their goal, they are part of a tradition that goes back hundreds of years and yet is as modern as the most experimental new ballet of today.

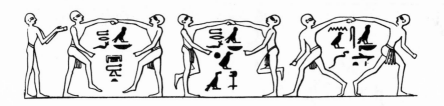

11. Modern Dance

Isadora Duncan, like Michel Fokine, felt that traditional ballet had become stale and artificial. Some even say that it was her appearance in Russia that inspired Fokine to launch his reforms. But Duncan did not try to change or reform ballet. Rather she went on to create a totally new type of dance, with few of the conventions and traditions of ballet.

Isadora Duncan (1878–1927) was born Dora Angela Duncan in San Francisco. Early in her career, a manager changed her name to Isadora. Her mother was a piano teacher, and Isadora and her sister, Elizabeth, would often dance to the Chopin and Mendelssohn pieces her mother played. It was free and expressive dancing. It did not use any of the steps or movements of ballet, which were largely unknown to the girls.

At first, Isadora and her sister danced just for the fun of it. But the two girls got so good at it that word of their talent spread. Soon they were giving dancing lessons to neighborhood children, and they were paid for the instruction.

Although she was already teaching, Isadora started to study ballet. But she found ballet rigid and formal and very different from her own developing concept of what dance

149

Isadora Duncan reacted against the staleness of nineteenth-century ballet by developing a completely new style of dance, which is now called modern dance.

should be. She stopped the lessons after just three classes and said later that those three classes were the full extent of her formal training in dance.

As she grew to consider herself a dancer, Isadora began creating dances to perform for others. The first pieces for which she made dances were the waltzes and mazurkas by Chopin that her mother played. She learned these dances and made the rounds of theater managers in San Francisco, hoping to find one who would present her in a dance recital. None showed the least bit of interest. Finally, Isadora and her mother, who was her accompanist, left San Francisco for Chicago, hoping to launch her career there.

In Chicago, too, there was no interest in Isadora's style of dancing. The little money they had when they arrived was soon gone. Isadora, therefore, felt compelled to accept an offer to dance in a vaudeville show being presented in a Chicago roof-garden restaurant. She was billed as "The California Faun." The owner forced her to add what she called "peppery stuff" and "frills and kicks," which went against all of her ideas on dance. After three weeks, she quit the restaurant job, even though she badly needed the money.

From Chicago, Isadora and her mother went to New York and started calling on theatrical agents and managers there. Again they had no success. She did, however, give several dance recitals and performed small roles in several musical shows. None of this satisfied Isadora, nor did it keep her far above starvation level. In 1899, Isadora decided to go to London to see if Europe would take more kindly to her dancing.

In London, and then in Paris, Isadora really began to develop as a professional. She read widely on dance and philosophy and clarified her own thinking on the purpose and meaning of dance. She visited museums, studying, in particular, the art of ancient Greece. She thought of how she could use the simplicity, the repose, the classical beauty, even the unadorned tunic and sandals, in her dances.

Another source of inspiration was the wavelike movement of ocean water, of wind, of flying birds, of bounding animals, even of mountain ranges. As she said, "all movements in Nature seem to me to have as their ground plan the law of wave movement." In the wave movement she saw a gradual build up of tension, a climax or crest, and a relaxation back to repose. Many of her dance movements sprang from wave movements and nature, but their aim was to evoke the spirit and rhythms of nature, not just to imitate it.

Isadora found, more and more, that the best way she could express her new concepts of dance was by using the natural human movements of walking, running, skipping, leaping, hopping, and falling. She discarded many of the steps, positions, and gestures that were part of the ballet tradition. "All the movements of our modern ballet," she said, "are sterile movements because they are unnatural." She dropped, also, the trappings of ballet—the toe shoes and the elaborate costumes and scenery. When she danced, she wore a simple, loose tunic, without shoes, and moved on a stage bare of scenery.

Isadora Duncan also searched within herself to find what she called, "the central spring of all movement, the crater of motor power, the unity from which all diversities of movement are born. . . ." She found it was not the base of the spine. Rather, it is the soul, which she defined as the source and seat of all emotions. The dancer's job, then, is to become fully aware of his or her soul and to let all dance movements flow naturally from this awareness.

As the "motors" to activate her soul, her emotions, and her dance movements, Isadora used musical works by the world's greatest composers. She did not try to "interpret" the music, nor to make the sounds "visual," as some of her imitators did. Rather she used the music to set her body into motion. She allowed its emotional content to add to the expressiveness of the dance.

The very first dance she created, in London, in February 1900, was to the music of Felix Mendelssohn's *Spring Song*. In her early years, Chopin, Schubert, Schumann, and Brahms were other favorite composers. Later she used Gluck, Wagner, and Beethoven. In her final years, she turned more

152

to Franck, Scriabin, and Tchaikovsky. Perhaps her most famous dance is to the music of Beethoven's Symphony No. 7—it took five years to create.

Isadora spent most of her life in Europe, performing in various countries on the Continent. She also established several schools to teach her ideas on dance to young girls, some of whom she adopted and gave her surname. Six of her students from Germany, nicknamed the Isadorables, had a very successful dance tour of the United States just after World War I.

While Isadora Duncan was forging a completely new approach to dance with great success, her personal life was beset with tragedy. Her wildly unconventional life and her many scandalous love affairs were the subject of much gossip. She had three children with two different men. One child died right after birth; the other two were drowned while still quite young when the car in which they were riding with their nurse plunged into the river Seine in Paris.

In 1922 Isadora married a Russian poet, Sergei Esenin. Three years later he committed suicide. And then, on September 14, 1927, as Isadora was about to go for an automobile ride in Nice, France, her long red scarf caught in the spokes of a wheel. When the car started forward, the scarf was yanked down, breaking her neck and killing her instantly.

The legacy that Isadora Duncan left behind is the creation of a major new art form, modern dance. She started with the same concerns as Fokine. Fokine reformed ballet from within. Duncan created a totally different type of dance.

While modern dance is a product of the twentieth century, its roots go back to primitive dance. Its goals are to express the dancer's innermost feelings and emotions. These responses dictate the movements. Modern dance uses ele-

In her dance *Soaring*, shown here as danced by the Joyce Trisler Danscompany, Ruth St. Denis carried forward Duncan's ideas. *Photo: John Dady; The Joyce Trisler Danscompany*

Clif de Raita dancing *Spear Dance Japonesque*, which was choreographed by Ted Shawn, a pioneer of modern dance. *Photo: John Dady; The Joyce Trisler Danscompany*

Duncan's ideas were further developed in such modern dances as *Dance in Space*, based on Doris Humphrey's 1920 choreography. *Photo: John Dady; The Joyce Trisler Danscompany*

ments of religious ritual to comment on and express basic human psychology and philosophy.

The first dancer to carry forward Isadora Duncan's ideas of modern dance was Ruth St. Denis (1877-1968), who added religious, ritualistic, and theatrical qualities to Duncan's pure movements. She was married to Ted Shawn (1891-1972), a leading male dancer, who was trying to develop a role for men in this new dance style. Together they formed the Denishawn Dance Company and School. In their active years, from about 1915 to 1930, they created a body of modern dance works and introduced modern dance to audiences by their many performances in the United States and abroad. Out of the Denishawn School came such major figures of modern dance as Doris Humphrey, Sophie Maslow, Charles Weidman, and the most famous of all, Martha Graham.

Martha Graham (born 1894) brought modern dance to an even higher level. After training at the Denishawn School and performing in its dance company, Graham formed her own company in 1929. She quickly became beloved and highly regarded as the leading dancer, choreographer, and teacher of modern dance. As a performer she had a commanding personality and an intensity that dominated the stage. As a choreographer, she devised a wide variety of movements and gestures as well as new ways of thinking about the body. The themes of her dances vary from explorations of human consciousness to evocations of life on the American frontier.

In recent times a number of original and imaginative performers and choreographers of modern dance have emerged. They have struck out in many different directions; using abstract dance movement, they have introduced humor, protested social injustice, and probed psychological difficulties.

Merce Cunningham is the "bad boy" of modern dance. After dancing with Martha Graham for five years, he formed his own company. Since leaving her company he has experimented with a wide range of dance effects, from having the dancers perform with their backs to the audience to determining the movements of the dance by chance. At first he was heckled or ignored, but now he is respected as a leading figure in the development of modern dance.

Before going off on his own, Erick Hawkins also danced with Martha Graham. His abstract dances use symbolism that is usually not related to the title of the work. He uses very advanced, modern music and décor, and insists on live musical accompaniment, instead of the recorded accompaniments some performers use.

One of the most active and popular modern dance groups is the Paul Taylor Dance Company. Taylor's choreography is strong and athletic and at the same time witty and humorous. *Three Epitaphs* is a good example of his dances that combine tragedy and comedy.

Twyla Tharp creates dances for her own modern dance company, as well as for ballet companies, such as the American Ballet Theatre and the Joffrey Ballet. Her music ranges from works by Joseph Haydn to Jelly Roll Morton and the Beach Boys. Although she is classical in her approach, there is a liveliness and energy that makes her dances appealing to audiences.

Dan Wagoner danced in Martha Graham's company and

Twyla Tharp's dance *Eight Jelly Rolls* is set to music by Jelly Roll Morton. *Photo: Tony Russell; Twyla Tharp Dance Foundation*

spent a period with Paul Taylor before he founded his own group. While many of his dances are humorous and whimsical, others are deeply emotional and expressive. The accompaniments to his dances vary from utter silence to a solo viola to bluegrass tunes.

Two dancer-choreographers, in particular, have brought their special talents to a wide variety of contemporary dance situations. Agnes de Mille (born 1909) started her career by giving solo dance recitals. In the 1940s, she choreographed the ballets *Rodeo* and *Fall River Legend*. Also during this same period she choreographed such Broadway musicals as *Oklahoma!, One Touch of Venus, Carousel, Brigadoon, Gentlemen Prefer Blondes*, and *Paint Your Wagon*. Her dances synthesized ballet, modern dance, and popular theater. They set a high standard for musical theater in America.

Jerome Robbins (born 1918) first danced professionally in Broadway musicals. He then performed with the Ballet Theatre, working his way up from the corps de ballet to soloist. He is credited with choreographing several works,

Sue's Leg is a lively, energetic dance choreographed by Twyla Tharp.
Photo: Tom Berthiaume; Twyla Tharp Dance Foundation

Dan Wagoner, shown here with Regan Frey, went on from Martha Graham's company to form his own. *Photo: Ron Reagan; Dan Wagoner and Dancers*

including *Fancy Free, Age of Anxiety,* and *The Cage.* From this work, Robbins moved to choreographing and directing such musical shows as *On the Town, The King and I, West Side Story,* and *Fiddler on the Roof.* Robbins has the wonderful gift of being able to incorporate the style and movements of ballet and jazz dance in his choreography for the theater.

As modern dance developed, a method of teaching this

159

Agnes de Mille's choreography for the Rodgers and Hammerstein musical *Oklahoma!* set a high standard for the theatrical dance. *The Lynn Farnol Group*

new style of dancing also developed. The approach differed from that used in teaching ballet.

Ballet teachers concentrate on passing on the traditional steps and movements; modern dance teachers concentrate on developing the concepts of space, time, and energy in dance. Ballet dancers work at the *barre;* modern dancers use the floor for their exercises. Ballet dancers wear slippers or toe shoes; modern dancers are barefoot. Ballet strives to combine and re-create the centuries-old movements; modern dance strives for creativity and improvisation. Ballet is somewhat restricted in the number of movements that are used; anything goes in modern dance.

Modern dance is taught in the same kinds of studios as ballet. Youngsters of almost any age can successfully start modern-dance training. At the beginning, they usually take a one-hour class each week, increasing the number as they grow older and become more advanced.

Several different basic approaches to modern dance are taught. Martha Graham, for example, advocates a focus on contraction, the pulling inward of the body, and on the release of muscle tension. The followers of Doris Humphrey use the act of falling and recovering as a central part of their technique. And the German dancer, Mary Wigman, devised a method based on the alternation of tension and relaxation.

Almost all modern-dance classes have the same four basic divisions. The first part of a class is devoted to work on technique. This is a time of warming up, of stretching and strengthening, of developing looseness and flexibility, and of

The *Dream Ballet,* choreographed by Agnes de Mille for the musical *Oklahoma!,* was a show stopper at every performance. *The Lynn Farnol Group*

learning basic movements. This is usually done standing, sitting, or lying down in the middle of the floor.

The second part teaches moving through space. The eight basic movements—walking, running, leaping, hopping, jumping, skipping, galloping, and sliding—are explored and tried with countless variations.

In the third area of concern improvisation and dance invention are investigated. The teacher gives the students various situations and problems to express in dance. "Listen to the music, and move in any way it tells you to move." "You have just heard some very sad news; show your feelings in a dance." "You have a heavy load on your back; make up a

Modern dancers often take striking positions as seen in this photo of the Pilobolus Dance Theatre's production of *Ocellus. Photo: Tim Matson; Pilobolus Dance Theatre*

dance that shows how it weighs you down." The students' job is to turn these words into dance movements.

The final part of the modern dance class often involves choreography. The students are guided in the creation of an original dance, based on some piece of music, a set of dance movements, or the telling of a story.

Since modern dance was, in part, a rejection of ballet, it was natural in the beginning of modern dance that the teaching methods of ballet would also be rejected. But, starting in the 1960s, ballet and modern-dance performers began to borrow from each other. And so, too, did the teaching methods become more alike.

In particular, modern-dance teachers are turning more to the positions, movements, and techniques of ballet instruction. *Barres, pliés, relevés,* and many other features of ballet are being used in modern-dance instruction. And the modern-dance techniques of improvisation, expressivity of movement, and creativity are finding their way into ballet teaching.

Twentieth-century ballet and modern dance were not only a reaction against the abuses of nineteenth-century ballet. They were also a response to the bewildering changes that were taking place in every phase of existence at the opening of the twentieth century.

Industrial production entered a period of growth and expansion. Factories grew in size and number as machines replaced workers and as mass production and the assembly line increased the speed of manufacture. Great quantities and varieties of goods were turned out quickly. Vast numbers of people left the farms to seek jobs in the factories. The gulf between the factory owners and the workers, between the rich and poor, grew ever wider. The socialist and communist ideas of Karl Marx, first stated in the mid-nineteenth century, were accepted by more people because of the

163

strained conditions. The Russian Revolution of 1917 was one of the many consequences of this social and economic upheaval.

In the years after the end of World War I in 1918, many of the old monarchies were overthrown and several new constitutional republics came into being. Among them were Russia, Germany, Spain, Poland, and Czechoslovakia.

In 1905 Albert Einstein's theory of relativity established new meanings for the terms *space* and *time*. These concepts had been the same for more than two hundred years, since the time of Sir Isaac Newton. Einstein showed that space and time were not absolutes but were related in ways that had never been conceived of by scientists in the past.

Painters, composers, dancers, and other artists worked to understand and express the new world that was evolving. Instead of trying to imitate reality in their paintings, artists revealed their feelings and ideas in nonrealistic, abstract art. Instead of following the rules that had guided the course of music for five hundred years, composers experimented with completely new melodies and harmonies.

In throwing over many of the traditions of the older dance forms of the past, the twentieth-century dance pioneers completely reformed ballet and created the new style of modern dance. The dancers who followed them and those who are performing today are similarly reflecting the economic, political, scientific, and artistic changes of *their* times.

12. Social Dance, Yesterday and Today

Up until about 1900, social dance in Europe and America was dominated by the waltz and a few other popular dances of European origin. In the early years of the century, the waltz began to slip from favor, as did the other European dances. New influences, mainly the music and dance of the black people in the United States and of the natives in South and Central America, began to reshape the social dances of the twentieth century.

As the century began, the order of the Old World, so perfectly symbolized by the waltz, began to crumble. There were also some lesser, more practical reasons for the decline of the waltz. In the early years of the century, dancing was an extremely popular pastime. Dance floors were always jammed, making it very difficult to do the turns and glides of the waltz, which need a great deal of space. Also, fewer German musicians, who had made up most of the best waltz orchestras in America, were available. In those years just before World War I, when the United States and Germany were preparing for war, many German nationals were returning home. And since popular sentiment was turning anti-German, restaurant and dance-hall owners were reluctant to hire German waltz orchestras.

Black Music and the Dance

Starting in the 1890s, in New Orleans, black people began developing a new style of music called ragtime or jazz. The original ragtime was probably played by Negro brass bands in street parades and funeral processions. It was based on march music. But instead of the usual ONE-two-THREE-four beat of the typical march, jazz players strongly syncopated the march rhythm, playing with a one-TWO-three-FOUR beat instead.

At the same time, black dancers in Florida were doing a dance believed to have been inspired by the war dances of the Seminole Indians. The dance started with couples walking in slow, solemn procession; the women in long white gowns carrying bouquets of flowers, the men in high collars and tails. Suddenly, they interrupted the walk for a gay dance interval, filled with jumping and shouting. Then, just as suddenly, they returned again to the dignified walk.

In time, there came to be contests for those who could walk or strut best in the promenade part of the dance. The traditional prize was a very large, heavily iced cake, which they were expected to share with the other participants. From this custom, the dance came to be known as the *cakewalk,* and the expression "That takes the cake" probably originated.

Black servants were sometimes invited to the fashionable balls of their employers to do the cakewalk. Northerners vacationing in Florida often attended these balls. They brought the idea of the dance home with them. The cakewalk quickly spread and became the dance craze in America in the final years of the nineteenth century.

Ragtime music and the cakewalk seemed made for each other. The frenetic rhythms and melodies of ragtime fit the frenzied interruption sections of the cakewalk perfectly. It

The cakewalk started with a slow, solemn procession, which was interrupted by gay dance intervals.

was the beginning of the close relationship between jazz and the social dances of the day.

From the grotesque, exaggerated interruptions in the cakewalk came a whole group of animal dances that were popular in the years around World War I. Among the best known were the *turkey trot, bunny hug, grizzly bear, kangaroo hop, camel walk, horse trot,* and *fish walk.* These wild dances were done almost as much for laughs as for the experience of dancing. And all of them were done to the new ragtime music.

Of all the animal dances, the one that emerged as the most popular was the *fox-trot.* In 1913, a comedian named Harry Fox opened his act on Broadway by strutting onstage in a step he called a trot. Because it resembled the other

Left: The man hugged the woman tightly in the dance known as the grizzly bear.

Below: The turkey trot was one of the popular animal dances of the early years of the twentieth century.

animal dances, or because it was Fox's dance, it came to be called the fox-trot.

As the fox-trot was taken up by many dancers, it became slower and more graceful. By 1914, only one year after its introduction, the fox-trot replaced the waltz as the most popular social dance. The music for the fox-trot was performed by jazz bands and later by dance bands and swing bands. The dance continues today to be a popular favorite, despite the many other dances that have come and gone.

The black rhythms of the 1920s also influenced the dance styles of the time. One of the first dances of the decade was the *shimmy,* or *shimmy shewabble.* Many eyebrows were raised at this dance in which the girls often performed with bare legs and in revealing costumes. In fact, in many cities police threatened to close any dance halls that allowed people to dance the shimmy.

Of all the animal dances, the fox-trot has remained the all-time favorite. *New World Pictures*

In a few years, the shimmy was replaced by the *Charleston*, which first appeared in a Broadway musical comedy in 1923. Within a year, the Charleston became the new dance rage. It came to symbolize the exuberance, energy, vigor, and vitality of that period. The popularity of the Charleston was challenged in 1926 by the *black bottom*. Alberta Hunter, who introduced the dance, insisted that the name referred to the dancers' movements, which suggested the dragging of feet through the dark, heavy mud on the bottom of the Suwannee River. There were many others, though, who felt sure it referred to the part of the body that was slapped during performances of the dance.

Very long dance contests, called dance marathons, were an important part of the dance scene during the 1920s. In these dances, prizes were awarded to the couples who danced longest without leaving the dance floor. The early dance marathons ended after fifteen or twenty hours of nonstop dancing. But the record was set by a winning couple in Somerville, Massachusetts, who danced from December 24,

The dance hit of the 1920s was the Charleston. *P/I's Dance Charisma*

Left: By the end of a dance marathon the exhausted dancers could barely stand up. *Cinerama*

Below: Although the jitterbug was first popular in the 1930s, some of its movements are still part of today's dances. *Photo: Melvin Berger*

171

The lindy is a dance that is similar to the jitterbug. It was named after Charles Lindbergh, the first pilot to make a solo flight across the Atlantic.

1932, to June 3, 1933, for a total of 3,780 hours. The rules allowed the dancers fifteen minutes of rest per hour at first. After twenty weeks, though, the dancers had only three minutes of rest per hour. And then they were not allowed to leave the floor at all until just one couple remained, which came after more than twenty-two weeks of nonstop dancing!

With the growing popularity of jazz and the happy, rhythmic, big-band sound of the swing music of the 1930s, a new dance emerged. It was called the *jitterbug*, the name coming from some unknown journalist who described the dancers as "jittering bugs." It was one of the most athletic dances of all time. Boys and girls did the jitterbug with widely contorted movements, which included the flinging of the girls up into the air by the boys.

A dance very closely related to the jitterbug was the *lindy*, which came a few years later. The lindy originated as the Lindbergh hop in 1927 to mark Charles Lindbergh's first successful solo flight across the Atlantic. Like the jitterbug, it was a very athletic and energetic dance.

172

Dances from South and Central America

Dances imported from South and Central America also helped to break up the traditional European dance patterns. In the 1890s, as the cakewalk was spreading from Florida to the rest of the country, a dance from Brazil, the *maxixe*, was making its way to the United States. The maxixe is a quiet dance, with much dipping and swaying from side to side.

The first really popular dance from South America, though, was the *tango*, from Argentina. It became known in the States around 1910. Some think that the tango was originally an African dance, brought to Argentina by African slaves. Still others believe that it was once a Spanish gypsy dance.

In any case, when the tango appeared in Argentina it was

Dances from South and Central America helped to break up the traditional European dance patterns. *MGM*

a favorite dance in the brothels. The woman's role in the dance was quite aggressive as she fought to hold on to her man. The man's role was to attack the woman and fling her about in an attempt to break free. The name comes from the Spanish word *tengo*, which means "I have," and refers to the woman's effort to keep the man.

As the tango was exported it was tamed and smoothed, and many of the sexual and sadistic elements in the dance disappeared. The tango today is a languorous, sophisticated dance, with sudden stops and hesitations. The steps are long and are performed with a proud, erect carriage.

Another Latin American dance hit of the 1930s was the

The rumba, from Cuba, combines elements of black slave dance and Spanish folk dance. *P/I's Dance Charisma*

After the tango was exported from Argentina, it became a languorous, sophisticated dance. *MGM*

The street dance rhythms of the samba were the inspiration for the ballet *Frevo,* choreographed by James Truitte. *Photo: Sandy Underwood; Cincinnati Ballet Company*

rumba, also spelled rhumba. This dance first appeared in Cuba, combining elements of black slave dance and Spanish folk dance.

The rumba originated as the miming of an animal courtship dance. Two barnyard fowls, represented traditionally by the woman wearing a long, ruffled skirt and the man wearing an elaborate ruffled shirt, circle and swoop around each other in stylized courtship movements.

Two more Latin American dances became popular at the end of the 1930s. The *conga* was a group dance that took its form from the early chain dances. The dancers form one long line with their hands on the hips of the person in front. The line then snakes its way around the floor to the characteristic 1-2-3-kick pattern.

The *samba*, introduced to the United States at the New York World's Fair of 1939, came from a black dance performed in Brazil at the beginning of Lent. As part of the celebration, the black Brazilians would march, sing, and play drums and rattles in an immense parade. Whenever the leader would call out "Samba," everyone would stop and improvise wild dance steps in place. The samba evolved from this custom of dance improvisation in the midst of a procession.

All in all, the period of the '30s was really another episode of dance mania. In addition to thousands of local dance bands, there were at least three hundred dance bands touring

The cha-cha was a Latin American dance introduced to the United States about 1955. *P/I's Dance Charisma*

the country and playing at restaurants, nightclubs, hotels, college dances, public dance halls, and anywhere else that people got together to dance.

During World II and the following years, though, social dancing went into a decline. There were fewer dance bands and dance halls. A few new Latin American dances were introduced in the '40s and '50s. Most notable were the *mambo*, *cha-cha*, *bossa nova*, and *merengue*. Still, there was a general waning of interest in dance.

In the early rock dances, the dancers stood in one place and moved to the heavily accented music. *Photo: Melvin Berger*

Rock 'n' Roll

Rock 'n' roll, born in the late 1950s, set the stage for a new burst of interest in dancing. The first dance to this new music was introduced in October 1961 at the Peppermint Lounge in New York City by a black entertainer, Chubby Checkers (real name, Earnest Evans, Jr.). Called the *twist*, it based its wiggling, twisting movements on the gyrating hips of rock's first star, Elvis Presley.

Although the twist is a couple dance, the dancers do not touch hands or embrace. They stand essentially in one place and respond to the music with independent gestures and movements involving the entire body, from head to toe.

The immense popularity of the twist led to the creation of many variations. All of them were based on the heavily accented beats of rock music. The *watusi* and the *swim* were dances that mimed the movements of surfing, a popular new sport in the early 1960s.

The *jerk*, which followed in 1965, was an even freer dance. The dancer raised one arm and then the other, bringing each one down sharply while snapping the head back. The jerks of the head induced dizziness and was not unlike the ecstasy-producing dances of primitive dancers. The *monkey* followed the jerk in short order. It took the arm movements of the jerk and used them to mime a monkey climbing a tree.

In the 1970s rock 'n' rollers started to dance in a new type of dance hall called a disco. Disco is short for discotheque, a French word for a place where records or discs are kept. Although in most discos people dance to recorded music, some discos feature live groups that play and sing. Discos grew in popularity during the '70s. By the late 1970s there were some two thousand discos in America, and new ones were opening each week.

In the disco dances, the couples respond to the music without following any set steps of patterns. *Photo: Melvin Berger*

Most of the disco dances have no rules, with no steps or movements to learn. They are much freer than any of the dances of the past. Anything goes. The dancers listen to the music and respond in any way they wish. Disco dances are mainly couple dances.

This new style of dancing seems to relate to the new attitudes that evolved during the '60s and '70s. Every institution, every form of authority, every convention of society was subjected to examination and challenge. A new wave of freedom swept the country. And just as people threw over many of the old rules and forms of behavior, so they stopped doing the old dance steps that had to be studied and learned.

180

People looked within themselves for a sense of identity and self-realization. The new dances reflect the independence, and sometimes the isolation, of this new spirit of self-discovery. Further, the equality of the sexes in the discos is surely a sign of the far-reaching impact of the women's movement on sexual liberation and equality.

A new type of disco dance, the *hustle*, appeared in 1972. It was first danced in the bars and nightclubs of El Barrio, the part of New York City where many people originally from Puerto Rico now live. Its music is based on the blues, but with a strong, prominent bass-guitar line.

What is very striking about the hustle is that it is a touching dance after years of nontouching rock dances. There are dips, spins, and breaks that must be learned and practiced to be done correctly.

The hustle is a touching dance that was introduced in the 1970s after years of nontouching rock dances. *P/I's Dance Charisma*

Is the hustle the beginning of a new trend in dancing? Is it a sign that the philosophy of the '60s and '70s is giving way to a different orientation? Are people reaching out to each other more than they did before?

It is still too early to say. But what is clear is that the hustle and the other dances of today are linked with the dances of the past and are part of an ongoing dance tradition that will continue far into the future.

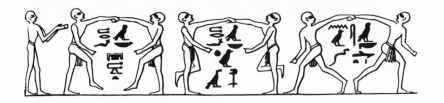

Bibliography

Dance History

Cohen, Selma Jeanne. *Dance as a Theatre Art.* New York: Dodd, Mead, 1974.

Kirstein, Lincoln. *Dance: A Short History of Classic Theatrical Dancing.* Brooklyn, N.Y.: Dance Horizons, 1969.

———. *Movement and Metaphor.* New York: Praeger, 1970.

Lawson, Joan. *A History of Ballet and Its Makers.* London: Pitman, 1964.

Meerloo, Joost A. M. *The Dance.* Philadelphia: Clinton, 1960.

Sachs, Curt. *World History of the Dance.* New York: Norton, 1937.

Sorell, Walter. *The Dance Through the Ages.* New York: Grosset & Dunlap, 1967.

Dance in Relation to Other Arts and Institutions

Hauser, Arnold. *The Social History of Art.* New York: Vintage, 1951.

183

Horst, Louis, and Russell, Carroll. *Modern Dance Forms in Relation to the Other Modern Arts.* Brooklyn, N.Y.: Dance Horizons, 1973.

Myers, Bernard S. *Art and Civilization.* New York: McGraw-Hill, 1957.

Sachs, Curt. *Commonwealth of Art.* New York: Norton, 1946.

Biographies

Duncan, Irma. *Duncan Dancer.* Middletown, Conn.: Wesleyan University Press, 1966.

Duncan, Isadora. *My Life.* New York: Liveright, 1972.

Fokine, Vitale. *Fokine.* Boston: Little, Brown, 1961.

Seroff, Victor. *The Real Isadora.* New York: Dial, 1971.

Terry, Walter. *Frontiers of Dance: The Life of Martha Graham.* New York: Thomas Y. Crowell, 1975.

General Books on Dance

Chujoy, Antole. *The New York City Ballet.* New York: Knopf, 1953.

Karsavina, Tamara. *Theatre Street.* New York: Dutton, 1961.

Martin, John. *World Book of Modern Ballet.* Cleveland: World, 1952.

Roslavleva, Natalia. *Era of the Russian Ballet.* New York: Dutton, 1966.

Sorell, Walter, ed. *The Dance Has Many Faces.* Cleveland: World, 1966.

Books of Dance Photographs

Krementz, Jill. *A Very Young Dancer.* New York: Knopf, 1976.

Swope, Martha. *A Midsummer Night's Dream.* New York: Dodd, Mead, 1977.

———. *The Nutcracker.* New York: Dodd, Mead, 1975.

Reference Works

Chujoy, Anatole, and P. W. Manchester. *The Dance Encyclopedia.* New York: Simon & Schuster, 1967.

McDonagh, Don. *The Complete Guide to Modern Dance.* Garden City, N.Y.: Doubleday, 1976.

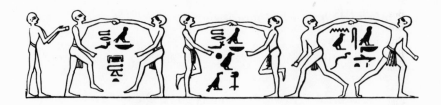

Index

Page numbers in italics indicate illustrations

187

188